Raising Baby Right

A Guide for
Avoiding the
20 Most
Common
Mistakes
New Parents
Make

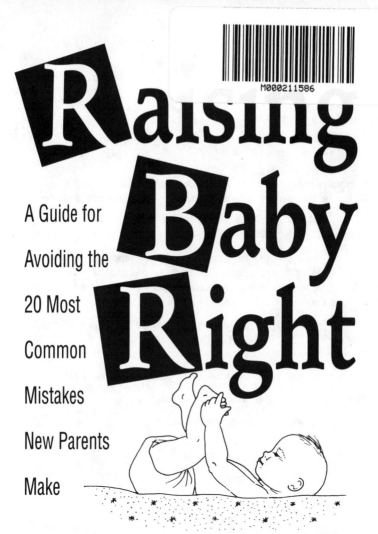

Charles E. Schaefer, Ph.D., and
Theresa Foy DiGeronimo, M.Ed.

Prince Paperbacks, New York

To our children, Eric S. and Colleen D., who will always be the "babies" in our families.

Although the authors have worked closely together to write *Raising Baby Right,* the first-person "I" who speaks to you throughout the book is the voice of Dr. Schaefer.

A Prince Paperback book. Published by Crown Publishers, Inc., 201 East 50 Street, New York, New York 10022. Member of the Crown Publishing Group.

Prince Paperbacks and colophon are trademarks of Crown Publishers, Inc.

Manufactured in the United States of America

Library of Congress Cataloging-in-Publication Data

Schaefer, Charles E.
    Raising baby right / by Charles E. Schaefer and
Theresa Foy DiGeronimo.
        p.   cm.
    Includes bibliographical references.
    1. Infants—United States.   2. Parenting—United States.
3. Infants—United States—Development.   I. DiGeronimo, Theresa
Foy.   II. Title.
HQ774.S33   1991
649'.122—dc20   91-548
                                                                      CIP

ISBN 0-517-58524-3

10 9 8 7 6 5 4 3 2 1

First Edition

Contents

Introduction

ongratulations! Whether you're reading this book to prepare for your baby's arrival or already have your newest family member settled comfortably in your home, we hope you'll accept this book as our way of reaching out to share your joy and give you a helping hand. We know from our experiences with our own children that each new arrival brings with him brand-new adventures in love and devotion, as well as in worry and anxiety. We hope this book will help you avoid some of the common mistakes that magnify the worrisome side of parenting and let you concentrate, instead, on the joyful side of getting to know your newborn.

One of the best ways to fully experience the bliss rather than the hardships of parenting is to learn how to avoid the stress triggers that can most easily upset you. It is the sole purpose of this book to help you do just that. Uncertainty, for example, is a trigger that makes us worry over things like: "Should I let my baby sleep in my bed?" "Should I pick up my crying baby?" Or, "Should my baby suck her thumb?" This book will answer these questions to help you feel more confident and, therefore, calm.

Overly ambitious goals are also stress triggers that can interfere with the joys of parenting. This book will help you choose realistic goals, set a daily pace you can live with, and allow you to lower your expectations of perfection without forfeiting your desire to be a good parent.

And finally, this book will point out the daily habits that put undue physical demands on you. It will give you permission and good reasons to take care of yourself so that after giving your all to your baby, you'll have some physical energy and emotional spirit left to give back to yourself and your spouse.

Parenting is the most demanding job in the world, but it also can be the most rewarding. It is our sincere hope that the information in this book will make it easier for you to reap these rewards in ample and unending supply.

Other books coauthored by Charles E. Schaefer and Theresa Foy DiGeronimo:

Toilet Training Without Tears
Teach Your Child to Behave
Help Your Child Get the Most Out of School
Winning Bedtime Battles

Ignoring the Symptoms of New Baby Stress Syndrome

At 6:20 A.M. two-month-old Mikey let out his first howl of the day. The call abruptly jolted Maureen from a deep sleep. "Oh, come on," she moaned to herself. "Give me a break." Maureen had been up to answer the baby's cries three times during the night and now she felt as if her body could not voluntarily stand up and walk into that nursery one more time. Making the move even more difficult was the thought of being stuck in the house on another winter's day only to change more diapers, offer more feedings, and again pass the hours pacing the floors burping and soothing. By four in the afternoon, Maureen had had it with the drudgery of parenting. "What's wrong with me?" she screamed in silence to herself as her tears fell down on her baby's face. "Why can't I take care of this baby I love so much without feeling so miserable?"

Obviously, Maureen is not experiencing what we call "baby bliss." But if we were to look back two months ago when she gave birth to her son, we'd see a very different picture. At that time she and her husband had a positive attitude and an optimistic outlook. They both knew there would be some adjustments and sacrifices to make, but they had planned for this baby and felt they were ready for the ups and downs that go with the responsibilities of parenthood. However, like so many other hopeful parents, Maureen was not at all prepared for the symptoms of what we call "New Baby Stress Syndrome" (NBSS), so she ignored them, assuming parenthood really was this awful.

WHAT IS NEW BABY STRESS SYNDROME?

New Baby Stress Syndrome is a group of symptoms commonly experienced by parents of newborns. It has its roots in the kind of stress we're all familiar with. Stress as you've experienced it in the past is an automatic physical reaction when you are faced with a new, unpleasant, or threatening situation. You have felt it if you've ever gotten a nasty office memo, or have been stuck in a traffic jam, or have become engrossed in a murder mystery movie. In response to these situations our heart beats rapidly, blood pressure rises, muscles tighten, palms perspire, and we may feel breathless. As an age-old survival response, these physical reactions gave our ancestors the extra strength needed to fight off danger or to flee from it. Even today, stress can be a positive thing because it keeps us alert to danger and inspires us to meet life's challenges. But prolonged or too-intense stress can wear down the body and show itself in illnesses such as ulcers, headaches, backaches, rashes, colitis, allergies, heart disease, diabetes, and (as found in the latest research) even cancer.

In addition to these common stress responses, many parents (like those quoted below) find that New Baby Stress Syndrome adds a few additional symptoms unique to the tensions of parenting. They include:

• **chronic tiredness**

"It never ends. Every time I think I've got everything done and I try to steal a minute to sit down and do nothing, the baby starts crying, or I realize I'm late for the baby's doctor appointment, or she spits out a mouthful of strained prunes, and I've got to start cleaning again. I can't remember what it's like to have a full night's sleep or even an ounce of energy."

• **feelings of being overwhelmed**

"I'm a pretty organized person, but since the baby was born, I can't get a routine going. I feel as if I spend my days running around going nowhere. It's so frustrating not to know what to expect next or where to start to even begin to make some kind of normal schedule."

• **reduction in self-esteem**

"I've always considered myself a competent person. Now when I talk to myself (and I do that a lot lately) I can't think of anything good to say. I'm constantly thinking things like 'You're so stupid.' Or 'Everybody else can raise children without falling apart, but not you.' I've even wondered if my baby would be better off being raised by somebody else."

• **decline in marital satisfaction**

"I know my husband's really upset that I don't have enough energy left at the end of every day to act interested in the details of his day (never mind have sex), but I'm not so impressed with him lately either. He knows I'm cooped up with this baby all day, and he still goes out after work with his friends. I thought he'd be more involved with the baby, you know, play with him and things like that, but he barely takes time to glance over and say, 'How ya doin',

sport?' Even if I had the energy, I just don't feel very loving toward him right now."

• **emotional outbursts**

"I don't know what happens, but all of a sudden I find myself either crying or yelling. I've even screamed at the baby to shut up when he was crying. The part of my brain that's still rational knows that screaming at an infant won't make him stop crying, but I do it anyway. And then there are days when I call the sitter from work to make sure everything's okay. When she tells me the baby is doing fine, I hang up and start crying. I've never acted like this before."

• **inability to relax**

"I'm always on duty. Twenty-four hours a day, I'm in charge of keeping this child content and healthy. Even when she's sleeping, I can't unwind; I keep thinking I hear her crying. At night, I don't really sleep; I feel as if I've always got one eye and one ear open— ready to jump into action."

Just as the symptoms of NBSS are varied, so are the causes. Some parents buckle under to emotional stress that's caused by unceasing worry about their child's welfare, and they sometimes compound this with self-doubt about their ability to be good parents. Some other parents suffer from extreme physical stress that can be caused by lack of sleep and poor nutritional habits—common by-products of trying to respond to the never-ending demands of a new baby. And still others struggle with psychological stress that strikes because they feel isolated, confused, and helpless. Whether Maureen's struggle with NBSS was caused by emotional, physical, or psychological stress, or a combination of the three, she shares a bond common to all parents who fall into its grip—difficulty cherishing and embracing the joys of parenting.

AVOIDING NEW BABY STRESS SYNDROME

Research continually documents what all parents quickly discover: Parenting is a very stressful occupation. Nothing can eliminate the stress because it's part of the parenting package and it's actually needed to alert you to danger and keep you on your toes. But to avoid the problems of New Baby Stress Syndrome, you need to know how to deal with the stress. Stress management can help you cope with the demands of your new lifestyle and allow you to concentrate more fully on the joys, the wonder, and the bliss of parenting. The following three stress-management guidelines will help you reach this goal.

Be Prepared

You will find more contentment in parenting if you can accept that, along with delight and happiness, your little bundle of joy will bring tension and uncertainty into your life. Knowing in advance that parenting is stressful will help you hold on to a positive attitude that will keep NBSS from your door.

If you find yourself feeling harried, lonely, or tense, don't react with self-recriminations such as "This is awful. I never knew taking care of this baby would be so hard. I can't stand this. Why do I have to have this kind of impossible child?" Instead, remind yourself that this is nothing more than "one of those days." Say positive things to yourself such as "Yes, this is awful, but I can get through this. I have a beautiful child. Someday I'll probably laugh about this." You'll find that being prepared with a positive attitude will ease your way through the sometimes dark periods of parenting.

Express Your Feelings

When the baby is crying and the doorbell is ringing and you can't find the pacifier, don't ignore or deny that you feel flustered. Negative feelings don't mean that you're not a good parent, so there's no reason to feel guilty when the day's events make you angry, unhappy, or hostile. When these feelings occur, say out loud, "I'm angry!" Or, "I hate staying with this baby all day." Or even, "I wish I never had this baby." Don't feel ashamed of yourself or add guilt on top of an already stressful time. There is nothing abnormal about these feelings; most parents experience them at some time. Those who keep them to themselves and ignore them or worry about being a bad parent for having such thoughts are prime candidates for NBSS; those who expect them, express them, and share them with sympathetic family and friends get past them and move on to the more positive aspects of parenting.

Learn to Relax

You can't get rid of parenting stress, but you can learn how to deal with it so it won't negatively change the way you feel about parenthood. The following stress-reduction techniques should help; they can be practiced on a regular daily basis or in times of emergency when you feel a stress overload. Because not all tactics work for all people, give each one a try and choose the ones that work best for you.

THOUGHT CONTROL: Thought control as a method of stress management is based on a very simple premise: When you talk to yourself, say something positive. When you hear yourself muttering resentful, loathsome, odious, or self-pitying thoughts, challenge them. Replace them with loving thoughts; recall moments with your baby when you felt the delight and wonder of parenthood, and pat yourself on the back for all the good things you've done for your baby. While you're doing this, *smile.* Smiling is a natural mood elevator that makes it difficult to hold on to stress. As you learn to manage stress, you'll find that control of your internal language is as important as your control of external factors.

DEEP BREATHING: Because the body needs oxygen to fuel its stress response, you can reduce the stress you feel by regaining control of your breathing. To stop the rapid breathing that accompanies a stress response:

• Take a deep breath from the bottom of your stomach. Feel it fill you with warm air.

• Breathe in as you silently count to five.

• Let the air go. Don't push it out. Let it go gently to the count of five.

• Do this sequence two times in a row.

• Then breathe regularly (rhythmically and comfortably).

• Deep-breathe again after you have let a minute or two go by.

• Repeat this deep-breathing/regular-breathing cycle two or three times, or as often as needed, until you find your breathing has returned to a natural and comfortable pace.

Deep breathing is a strategy you can use anywhere, anytime to change your body's reaction to stress.

GUIDED IMAGERY: Guided imagery allows you to retreat to an internal world where you feel safe and relaxed whenever you imagine yourself being there. This approach is based on the belief that imagining a positive experience can stop or prevent a stress reaction.

To practice guided imagery, think of a place that you find totally relaxing. Create this place so it is completely nonstressful—no crying babies, no harsh winds, no responsibilities. You might, for example, imagine yourself lying, with your eyes closed, on the warm sands of some faraway beach. You feel the sun gently warm your skin, and you hear in the distance the rhythmic sound of the tide's ebb and flow. You reach your hand into the sun-heated sand and you let the grains sift through your fingers. In your special place, stress can't find you.

Wherever you decide to build your relaxing place—be it in the woods, at the park, by a lake, or in your own home by the fireside—practice going there often. The more familiar you are with the details of this place, the more readily you will be able to imagine it when you're feeling stressed.

New Baby Stress Syndrome is not an inevitable curse cast upon all new parents. But if you should notice that you're finding less and less enjoyment in the time you spend with your baby, don't ignore the symptoms. Use the advice and information we've gathered together in this book to help you sidestep the pitfalls of parenting a baby, deal with its stress, and focus more fully on the joys of being a parent.

Hesitating to Comfort a Crying Baby

E va nervously washed the dishes as her husband, Raphael, kept himself busy fixing a sliding cabinet door that had fallen off the track. Both were trying to ignore the screams of one-month-old Sarah coming from the bedroom down the hall. "I can't stand hearing her cry," sighed Eva. "It makes me feel so cruel."

"I know," agreed Raphael. "But you know we can't go and pick her up every time she cries. She's dry and fed and there's nothing wrong with her. If we pick her up she'll expect us to do it all the time and we'll end up with a spoiled baby who cries to be picked up all day long."

"I know. It's better for all of us in the long run, but right now it's so hard."

Eva and Raphael have heard from relatives and friends that if they pick up their crying baby, they'll spoil her. So, in an attempt to do what's right, they occasionally let her cry. This is a very common mistake that leaves both the baby and the parents feeling insecure and stressed.

The fact is: For the first six months, it is unlikely you will spoil your baby by swiftly responding to each cry or by surrendering to your impulse to cuddle and comfort. During this time many babies need a great deal of comforting to help ease the transition between intrauterine and independent life. Also, these babies do not have the ability to make the mental connection that enables older children to reason, "If I cry, I'll get my own way." Infant cries can, and should, be answered.

THE SOUNDS OF CRYING

Babies often cry to communicate a need. Research studies have found that, with practice, many parents can more effectively respond to babies' needs when they learn to tell what an infant wants by the sound of the cry. The following descriptions of crying patterns may help you zero in on the cause, and therefore the remedy, of your baby's crying.

Hunger

Babies say, "I'm hungry" with a rhythmic cry that repeats a cry-pause-cry-pause pattern. The sound is less shrill than other cries and sounds demanding rather than desperate. This cry is often preceded by finger sucking, lip smacking, or breast nudging. If the baby stops crying when picked up, it's not a hunger cry.

Tiredness

Babies react to fatigue with a cry that has a wailing sound and a definite vibrato. This cry gradually builds in intensity and often has a continuous and nasal quality.

Boredom

Babies say, "I'm lonely and bored" with a cry that is whiney and whimpering; sometimes it almost sounds like a moan. This cry stops abruptly when the infant is picked up.

Illness

Sick babies signal their discomfort with a prolonged cry. The cry sounds whiney and nasal. It is generally lower in pitch than a pain cry. The cry can more readily be identified as a signal of illness when it is considered together with changes in the baby's appearance and behavior. He or she may have a flushed face, appear listless, refuse to eat, have diarrhea, and avoid cuddling.

Pain

Babies in pain generally bring attention to their discomfort with a cry that begins suddenly and is high-pitched and shrill. The cry is loud and long (as long as four seconds) and is followed by a lengthy pause of breath-holding (as long as seven seconds). The baby may wake from sleep with a screamlike cry; the mouth will open wide, the lips may turn blue or purple, and the tongue may turn upward. Arms and legs may flail and then jerk tensely back into the body. This cry is nonstop and inconsolable. Infants who are ill or in pain will continue crying despite your efforts to soothe. If you suspect your baby's crying is caused by a medical problem, be sure to call your doctor immediately.

Prolonged Crying

COLIC: Colic crying is different from other kinds of crying. It is usually easily identifiable because it generally occurs like clockwork every afternoon or evening, lasts for several hours each time, and is not stopped for long by anything. Soothing a colicky baby can sometimes require special tactics, which are explained in Mistake #3.

IRRITABILITY: Irritable babies cry on and off all day long and often wake crying during the night as well. The causes of this irritability are speculative, but research has found several probable factors including: maternal stress during pregnancy (such as divorce or death in the family), drug abuse by the expectant mother, food allergy, hypersensitivity (a tendency to startle at the slightest sound or touch), or hyperarousal (immature regulation of the central nervous system, which causes sleeping difficulties).

Soothing techniques may work better with these babies than with colicky ones. But because irritable babies can often cry as much as twelve hours a day, most parents find it absolutely necessary to let them cry it out occasionally. In fact, because it is so difficult to soothe these babies, it seems likely that, for some infants, the crying serves some vital purpose. (See Mistake #4 for information about "crying it out.")

SOOTHING THE CRY

It takes many parents a while to learn the different sounds of crying, and sometimes even the most experienced moms and dads simply can't tell what's making the baby cry. On these occasions when you can't figure out what your baby wants, you might want to try some common soothing techniques. When you do, remember these general guidelines:

1. When your baby cries, go to him as soon as you can. A baby who gets "worked up" in hysteria is much harder to soothe.

2. Check for obvious causes of discomfort. Is the baby dry? fed? warm? et cetera.

3. Use the trial-and-error method to discover which of the techniques explained below best soothe your baby.

4. Even if your baby continues crying while you try to soothe, continue using the chosen method for at least ten minutes. It often takes that long for an infant to realize what you're doing.

5. If after ten minutes the chosen method isn't working, try another one for another ten minutes. Keep this up until either your baby is calm or you feel as if you need a break. Then it's time to find someone else to calm your baby or for you to let the baby cry (see Mistake #4).

SOOTHING TECHNIQUES
Physical Contact

Pick up and cuddle your baby as often as you like. Remember, for the first six months, you will not spoil your baby by giving her too much attention. In fact, babies whose cries are answered promptly in the first three months tend to cry less later on than those whose newborn cries were often ignored.[1] If your baby calms when you carry her, but you can't carry the child all day long and get anything else done, you'll find that an infant sling may be the perfect solution to the problem. These baby carriers hold the baby close to your body, encourage bonding, will often stop the crying while enabling you to use your arms, and give you more freedom to move around and get on with your own activities. They also offer dads a unique chance to keep their babies close to their bodies.

Rhythmic Motion

Many babies stop crying when in motion. Rocking chairs, baby swings, carriage rides, waltzes across the floor, and car rides are all modes of movement that calm many wailing babies. If your baby seems readily soothed by a car ride, you might want to invest in a device called Sleep-Tight®. This is a crib attachment that simulates the feeling of an automobile traveling at fifty-five miles per hour. Because this crib vibrator has been classified as a medical device by the FDA, it may be covered by your medical insurance. You should, however, check with your pediatrician before investing. (To order, call Sweet Dreams, Inc., 1-800-NO-COLIC.)

Swaddling

Swaddling in a lightweight receiving blanket often restores a newborn's sense of comfort and closeness. That's why babies are routinely swaddled in hospital nurseries to reduce their fearful crying. To swaddle at home, take one corner of a receiving blanket and fold it down six inches. Place the baby on the blanket with his head above the fold. Next, take one side of the blanket and draw it across the baby's body. Fold the bottom section up over the baby's feet, then fold the last section across his body. Finally, turn the swaddled baby onto his stomach. If the baby cries harder after swaddling, don't persist. Some babies find it too confining.

Noise

Run the vacuum cleaner near your baby to provide a constant humming sound. The static of the radio off channel, the hum of a laundry washer or dryer, or a tape recording of a waterfall, running shower, or heartbeat are all sounds that parents have found will calm a fussing baby.

Comfort Sucking

Some babies have strong sucking needs that are not related to their desire for food. Their crying is often controlled by sucking on their fingers or fist or a pacifier. Time-tested tips for successful pacifier use include: give the baby the pacifier before she reaches a screaming pitch, and, to avoid tooth decay, don't sweeten the nipple with honey. (See Mistake #9 for a fuller discussion of pacifier use.)

Singing

Even if you can't carry a tune, singing in a melodic and calm refrain may have magical soothing powers. Frank R. Wilson, a neurologist and coeditor of *Music and Child Development,* says that babies come to associate certain sounds and melodies, such as lullabies, with parental love and security. When a child is upset, these melodic sounds can provide reassurance by creating a sense of emotional security.[2] So sing to your baby often to help him build this association that will provide you with an always-available source of comfort.

Relief Help

On those days when nothing will soothe your crying baby, you may need to hand her over to someone else. Constant crying is bound to make you feel tense and angry; these feelings are picked up by your infant, who then cries all the more. You may be surprised when your spouse, or a friend, or a grandmother cradles your "inconsolable" baby and magically calms the screams. Use that time to take a break and calm your nerves for a while.

Sometimes, NOTHING will soothe a crying baby. Persistent crying may be caused by colic (discussed in Mistake #3), or it may be that your baby just needs to have a good cry (as explained in Mistake #4). But before you throw up your hands in distress, give these soothing techniques a try. Most often, one of them will do the trick.

Recommended for further reading:

79 Ways to Calm a Crying Baby
Diana S. Greene
Pocket Books, 1988

Despairing over Colic

Brian tiptoed into the kitchen and noiselessly eased himself into the chair. With fingers crossed he and his wife, Donna, began to eat their dinner. Several uninterrupted bites of a meal seemed too good to be true. Relaxing, enjoyable dinners had become a thing of the past in this household since newborn Sean arrived. Every night as dinner was served, Sean began a screaming routine that continued just long enough to ruin dinner, upset any attempt at conversation, obliterate TV viewing, and get his parents tied up in knots of tension and frustration. Nothing could stop him—not feeding, rocking, singing, bouncing—nothing. As Brian started to butter his bread, he heard a stirring sound coming from the nursery. He and Donna froze and waited for the baby's next move. Then it came—the shriek that signaled the onset of their parental nightmare—evening colic.

WHAT IS COLIC?

Colic is a broad term used to label a condition that has no truly specific diagnosis. Most pediatricians will say an infant is suffering from colic when long crying episodes occur at predictable times every day and when nothing soothes the cry for more than a few minutes. Before colic is diagnosed, a pediatric checkup is necessary to rule out illness or physical problems that could cause such excessive crying. Surprisingly, there is usually nothing "wrong" with a colicky baby; this infant is thriving and gaining weight.

Like most colicky babies, Sean's crying bouts began when he was about one week old, and now each night at the same time he suddenly begins to cry and soon reaches a screaming pitch. As he cries, his elbows are bent, hands are clenched, and legs are usually tightly drawn against his tense and sometimes distended abdomen. He holds his breath for brief periods and often passes gas. This poorly understood symptom complex, which causes great distress for infants and parents, affects about 20 percent of all babies. If misery truly loves company, the parents of colicky babies can feel comforted knowing they are not alone.

CAUSES OF COLIC

In the past, colic has been attributed to numerous causes. Some theories include: hyperactive colon, excess gas, allergies to milk, an immature digestive system, birth complications, hormone deficiency, innate temperament, immature central nervous system, and nervous or unhappy parents. In truth, colic is probably a unique combination of several of these causes that are individual to each baby.

Because colicky babies pass gas and draw up their legs as if in pain, colic is commonly associated with dietary problems. Many medical experts hesitate to agree, however. If colicky babies have excess gas, they feel, it's probably because they have gulped so much air while screaming. More specifically, a recent study by Dr. William Treem of Hartford Hospital in Connecticut found that colicky babies had about the same amount of gas as a control group of babies without colic.[1] Many others try to draw a relationship between colic and the baby's diet. Some breastfeeding mothers eliminate foods from their own diets that they feel may be upsetting their babies. Other mothers switch formulas looking for one that will ease their baby's pain. Unfortunately, most studies have found that although dietary changes may reduce crying for a few days, the excessive crying soon returns and further frustrates hopeful parents.[2]

Some physicians prescribe medication to reduce colic crying. Sedatives, sedatives in combination with other drugs, and agents that attempt to regulate gastrointestinal function or reduce intestinal spasms are sometimes used to "cure" colic. However, the majority of pediatricians hesitate to give infants these drugs because the true cause of the crying is not clearly known. Also, there is little data to support the effectiveness of drug therapy in the

treatment of colic.³ So perhaps the medication is more often pre-
scribed for the infant to soothe the nerves of the parents.

When the pediatrician can find nothing physically wrong with a
crying baby, many parents worry that they are the cause of their
baby's distress. However, you will find yourself in a no-win situation if you worry that your own anxiety or tension is causing your
baby's colic. It's true that babies do react negatively to a parent's
tension. So, the more you worry that you are the cause of the
crying, the more your baby will cry. Don't put the blame on
yourself! Keep in mind that parental tension alone is an unlikely
cause because a baby's negative reaction to parental anxiety usually
doesn't happen at the same time every night as colic does. Also,
studies show clearly that not every baby with colic has upset
parents, so it is obviously not the sole cause.

LOVING A COLICKY BABY

Although your own worries may or may not contribute to your
baby's colic, excessive crying can certainly affect how you and your
baby react to each other. It's hard to feel affectionate toward an
infant who will not respond to your efforts to comfort and nurture.
The anger and frustration that build during the daily colic period
often carry over into a general attitude about parenting. Many
parents of colicky babies grow depressed and feel completely inept;
then they suffer the guilt caused by their cold and unloving feelings.
As a result, the babies of these parents lose out on some of the
cuddling and loving interaction they need. It's not your baby's fault
that she cries every day, but it's also understandable why it's so
difficult to stand idly by and just listen to the screams without
becoming frustrated and angry.

If your baby has colic, before you throw up your hands in
despair, you should try to find some way to calm the noise. Dr.
Bruce Taubman, author of *Curing Infant Colic,* suggests that parents first consider the five most common reasons for infant crying.
Try to find out if your baby needs to be 1. fed, 2. put to sleep, 3.
offered opportunity for sucking, 4. held, or 5. stimulated.⁴ If you
find that the child does not want food, will not go to sleep, refuses
the pacifier, doesn't calm when held, and doesn't respond to a

change of scenery, you should then try additional soothing techniques explained in Mistake #2. They may not work for long or
every day, but when they do, you'll feel satisfied that you've done
something, and your baby will enjoy the reprieve from tears.

TAKING CARE OF YOURSELF

The constant cry of a colicky baby is sometimes simply unbearable.
So how is a new parent to cope with this frustrating situation that
has no solution? There is no quick or easy answer to this question,
but surely some sturdy strands of sanity can be salvaged if you think
ahead during the quiet times of the day. Plan how you'll handle the
crying when it starts and, very important, how you'll talk to yourself
when your nerves start to become frazzled.

Expect the crying. If your baby has colic, one thing you can
count on is that he or she won't skip an evening of screaming. Don't
plan to have dinner, or visitors, or quiet conversations during this
time. Plan to spend part of the colic period practicing soothing
tactics, but also acknowledge that you can't stand on your eyelashes
to calm this child for three hours on end without becoming overwhelmed with anger. You'll need to plan how to handle your own
tension when the going gets tough: Before you reach the end of
your patience, put your baby down to cry for ten or fifteen minutes.
Try to spend this time calming yourself—do the stress-relief exercises previously listed, or if someone else can take charge, take a
walk or a shower so you can't hear the screams. Then go to your
baby and cuddle for a few minutes; again try favored soothing
tactics. If the baby continues to cry, put him down for another ten
or fifteen minutes, and again calm yourself. It isn't easy to let your
baby cry, but parents of colicky babies soon learn that sometimes,
in the name of survival, it's necessary.

Don't blame yourself. There are far too many factors involved
to take sole responsibility for colic. Neither you nor your spouse
should let these periods of crying convince you that you are inadequate parents. While your infant is wailing, remind yourself over
and over again that this is not your fault. You have done nothing to
cause the crying. You are a good parent.

Take a break. All parents of colicky babies need time out. Encourage your spouse to share the responsibility by taking turns using soothing tactics and arrange for a sitter on a regular basis so you can get away from your baby. As odd as it sounds, the growth of a positive relationship with your baby may depend on how often you can get away from her. During this relief time don't clean the house or do the bills—relax! Do things you enjoy such as taking a walk, visiting a friend, or sitting in the bath.

Don't forget that colic is temporary. Like pregnancy, colic, too, is a stage of growth and development that will end. Typically, the crying periods peak at six weeks of age and then taper off by four months. Eventually *all* children grow out of colic. However, if after six months of age your baby continues to cry inconsolably at predictable times each day, be sure to double-check with your pediatrician. The child may be suffering from a food allergy or physical problem that was not initially obvious.

Lastly, always remember that crying will not physically or psychologically harm your baby. This is perhaps the hardest lesson of all to learn because it's so difficult for parents to let their babies cry, even when it is apparent that nothing is going to stop the crying. The information in the next chapter will help you better understand why sometimes you can safely let your baby "cry it out."

Recommended for further reading:

Curing Infant Colic
Bruce Taubman
Bantam, 1990

Letting Crying Make You Crazy

S ince Kaitlyn's birth one month ago, Sara has tried "everything" to make her stop crying. "I don't mind when Katie cries because she's hungry or wet," Sara confesses, "but when she keeps crying even when I know she's full, dry, and not in any pain, it just drives me crazy!" Sara has what she calls a "walk me, rock me, bounce me" baby who is happy only when she's in Sara's arms. Although Sara laughs when she describes how she can now wash the dishes, do the laundry, make the beds, and brush her teeth with only one hand while she holds Kaitlyn in the other, the day-to-day ordeal of carrying around a crying baby is no laughing matter. Like so many other caring parents, Sara is tired, confused, overwhelmed, and frustrated in her attempts to keep her baby from crying. Although she's making a gallant attempt, the effort is often a mistake.

Sometimes, for reasons that have nothing to do with good or bad parenting, babies are inconsolable. And sometimes because parents are humans, we are too tired or too busy to devote every breathing second to the task of making our babies happy. Given that we can't always stop the crying, we can probably better handle the stress it causes when we learn that infant crying is not always a dilemma that needs a solution or an illness that needs a cure. Very often, crying is a natural and necessary part of infancy that cannot always be muffled.

SURVIVAL OF A CRYING BABY

A child's first voice serves as a survival mechanism that guarantees attention. *The sound* of a baby's cry has, for example, been shown to release milk in breastfeeding mothers. It is also an innately aversive and distressing sound that's tough for any parent to ignore. As the loudest sound a human can make (equal to an unmuffled truck in your living room!), crying causes parents to experience physical reactions such as rapid, shallow breathing, increased heart rate, and rising blood pressure. No wonder we jump to attention and will try anything to stop the sound.

Several surveys have found that parents quickly attend to crying babies for a number of reasons. Some run to their screamers because they feel an instinctive need to comfort and to relieve what is perceived as distress. Others respond to relieve their own distress because they find the sound too unpleasant to bear. Still others (most of us, we suspect) walk the floors and pay the price of fatigue and frustration because of feelings both for the baby and for ourselves.

CRYING CHART

DIRECTIONS: Use the chart below to keep track of how often your baby cries each day. Shade in each block of time that represents a crying period. Do this for at least four days to give yourself an adequate average sampling. If the total crying exceeds the averages listed on page 29, show this chart to your pediatrician; it will help him or her determine possible causes for the crying. If your baby's crying time falls within the expected averages, you'll be better able to accept the crying objectively as "normal" rather than excessive. You can also use this chart to help determine your baby's crying patterns that signal periods of fatigue, boredom, or hunger.

	AM												PM											
	12	1	2	3	4	5	6	7	8	9	10	11	12	1	2	3	4	5	6	7	8	9	10	11
DAY 1																								
DAY 2																								
DAY 3																								
DAY 4																								
DAY 5																								
DAY 6																								
DAY 7																								

Regardless of your reason for attending to your baby's cries, you'll soon learn that the effort can sometimes be extremely discouraging. More than any other aspect of parenting, an infant's inconsolable crying can make new parents feel frustrated and inept. Surely, we reason, we must be doing something wrong. Maybe, we wonder, we don't have what it takes to be good parents. Or perhaps, in our darkest moments, we conclude that the baby is simply obnoxious and spoiled. Before you throw your hands up in despair and decide that either there's something wrong with you or your child is "impossible," there are a few facts about crying that you should know.

CRYING TIME

All healthy, normal babies cry. In fact, several studies have found that the average daily crying time progresses in rather predictable developmental stages. At one week of age, infants cry a total of approximately 1 hour in each twenty-four hour period; at two weeks you can expect crying time to increase to 2 hours; crying time generally peaks at six weeks, with most babies clocking a total of about 2.75 hours. Then by twelve weeks of age, the babies return to their more bearable one hour crying time.

It may seem that your child cries much more than these averages ("all day long" is how many parents calculate crying time), but if you keep a record form (like the one provided on page 28) and note the actual length of crying jags, you'll probably be surprised to find that, although minutes seem like hours, the total time is at or close to average. Although most parents can accept this fact intellectually, it's a lot tougher to accept normal crying when you've tried "everything" to stop it.

LETTING THE BABY CRY

After a period of trial-and-error, you'll soon find which techniques listed in Mistake #2 best soothe your baby. And although you'll want to comfort your baby whenever you can, like all parents you'll also find that there will be times when, no matter what you do, you simply can't stop the crying. This is especially so when the baby's normal, daily crying time increases (as explained above) and you begin to worry it's because of something you did or something you didn't do. You should prepare yourself in advance of these times to accept an increase in crying as normal and to give your baby the freedom he may need to cry it out occasionally.

Some parents have a hard time letting babies cry. How would you feel if you wanted to take a shower, but every time you put the baby down she started to scream—would you take the shower anyway? Would you feel guilty and neglectful if you returned from the basement where you were doing laundry to find that your baby had been crying the whole time you were gone? Would you be embarrassed enough to leave the playground if your baby began to wail inconsolably?

Parents who can't let their babies cry sometimes find it most difficult to handle the stress of parenting. In fact, in one study of child abuse in children under one year of age, excessive crying was given as the reason for battering by 80 percent of the parents.[1] Other studies have found crying to be the primary reason for Shaken Baby Syndrome—a medical condition brought on by roughly shaking a child. This shaking can cause brain damage and bleeding as well as spinal cord and eye damage. To handle the stress of a crying baby, all parents need to learn more about the positive and necessary aspects of infant crying.

Most of us do find it difficult to let a baby cry, but as the following information documents, you shouldn't feel bad, guilty, or inept when your baby cries—in fact, sometimes you should let him.

Crying for Life

At birth, crying speeds the baby's transition from fetal circulation to independent pulmonary oxygenation. In utero, the fetus "breathes" through the umbilical cord, which carries oxygenated blood to all the infant's body systems. At the moment of birth, the robust cry of a healthy infant brings oxygen into the child's lungs, where it is sent into the blood stream to support life independent of the mother. In these moments after birth, crying is one of the factors used to determine the Apgar score, which is used to evaluate the baby's overall condition. So, instead of viewing crying as a sign of weakness, you can interpret it as an indicator of health and alertness.

Crying and Speech Development

Crying can enhance speech development. What may sound to you like nothing but noise actually provides babies with some awareness of their lips, tongue, palate, jaw, and voice. It exercises their vocal cords and gives them practice at vocalizing. The importance of crying to speech development is evident in the impaired speech of deaf babies. It has been found that at about three months of age, their crying starts to subside. They don't hear their own voice, and as a result, their speech development is disrupted.

Crying to Relieve Tension

Call to mind the methods you use to relieve tension. Do you take a walk? Call a friend? Turn on soothing music? Meditate? Well, babies also experience tension each day, but can't let off steam in one of the more socially acceptable modes that you can, so they cry. Because babies have an immature central nervous system, they become easily overstimulated by many seemingly normal day-to-day activities like an outing to the park, a visit from an aunt who talks loudly, or a day of errand running. To calm the stress, some babies need to have a good cry. The more their parents try to soothe their outbursts by rocking, walking, or talking, the more stimuli the babies need to process and the further overwhelmed they feel. Like all of us, sometimes babies just need to cry. T. Berry Brazelton, M. D., professor emeritus of pediatrics at Harvard Medical School, has often explained his belief that crying gives very stimulated babies a way to blow off steam. As a baby grows and matures, this crying gradually decreases as she learns how to discharge tension in other ways. The good news about this tension-relief crying is that it usually stops at ten to twelve weeks of age.

Scientists are just now finding why we sometimes feel better after a good cry. It seems that the chemical makeup of physical tears (the kind caused by irritants such as pollen and raw onions) is different from that found in emotional tears (the kind caused by feelings such as sadness). The chemicals found in emotional tears are similar to the physical substances the body makes to fight pain and manage stress. Because crying releases these substances, it actually *can* make us feel better.

If your baby becomes completely inconsolable and you're too tired, irritable, or busy to continue juggling soothing strategies, don't make the mistake of letting the crying make you crazy. Once you're *sure* that the baby is not ill and there's nothing more you can do to stop the wailing, calm yourself and give both you and the baby a break from each other.

As parents of colicky babies must sometimes do, put the baby down, close the door behind you as you leave, and let your screamer have a good cry for ten or fifteen minutes. This will seem like an eternity if you stand by the room and listen or if you watch the clock tick through each excruciating minute. Go to a part of the house where you can't hear the crying, or do some vacuuming while wearing earphones, or take a shower. Keep reminding yourself of crying's positive side. After ten or fifteen minutes, go to your baby and cuddle for a few minutes, and offer a water bottle if you like. If the baby continues fussing, put him down again and repeat the procedure over and over again until the crying stops.

Infant crying is normal. Knowing, at the very least, that nothing awful or harmful is happening to a crying baby while you take a shower, change your clothes, or just take a break should help you stop feeling guilty and stressful every time you can't stop your baby's tears.

Recommended for further reading:

Teach Your Baby to Sleep Through the Night
Charles Schaefer and Michael Petronko
Signet, 1987

Jumping into Bonding

Barbara's labor had been long and difficult. She and her husband, Tom, had put in eighteen hours of breathing exercises that left them both exhausted but jubilant when their son finally arrived weighing in at seven pounds fourteen ounces. Their joy was shortlived, however, when the nurse placed the newborn child into Barbara's waiting arms. For months Barbara and Tom had imagined how special this moment would be—the moment of bonding that would seal a loving and secure relationship with their child. Barbara looked at her son and felt only nausea; the long hours of pain and anxiety were taking their toll. Tom looked at his son and felt a sense of repulsion. The baby was still covered with a thin white film; his head seemed elongated and his face looked more like a moldy wrinkled potato than a vision of blessed beauty. Without saying a word to each other, Barbara and Tom began their career in parenting feeling guilty and inadequate.

WHAT IS BONDING?

Parent/child bonding is a complex process in which a parent and a child develop a strong emotional attachment. The term *bonding* is a bit misleading, however, because it gives the impression of an epoxy glue–type union that, in a moment's time, adheres two beings together forever. That's not at all what bonding is about. Human bonding is a gradual process that begins before a child's birth and continues throughout childhood.

Some people believe that there is a "critical" bonding period immediately after birth. This notion leaves many new parents like Barbara and Tom feeling guilty and depressed when in the moments after childbirth they feel little more than exhaustion and a vague sense of fondness toward the newly arrived child. Quite commonly, truthful women admit, "I thought it would be love at first sight, but when I first looked at my son, 'love' was hardly my reaction." This idea of instant bonding is also quite upsetting to adoptive parents who are not available to the child immediately after birth. It's equally distressing to parents who are separated from their babies because either the baby or the mother needs prompt medical care.

Fortunately for these parents who worry they've missed their chance to form a lasting attachment to their child, bonding does not happen in an instantaneous and magical moment. It happens each day in the routine interactions between a parent and a child. Not in the perfunctory acts of feeding and changing diapers, but in the smiles, coos, and moments of eye contact that occur during these activities. It happens as parents learn about and respond to their baby's patterns, temperament, likes and dislikes, and unique daily rhythms. And it happens as babies become aware of their parents' smell, sound, and touch.

Bonding doesn't occur instantly, but it is very important that the process does occur. A secure parent/child relationship forms the basis for all later emotional attachments and it lays the groundwork that will enable the child to seek and achieve loving and secure relationships in adult life. Emotional attachment also contributes to the infant's overall mental and physical growth. Studies repeatedly find that babies who are deprived of the opportunity for emotional attachment are at risk for suffering the Failure-to-Thrive Syndrome. This is a collection of symptoms that occur for no apparent physical reason; they include loss of weight, failure to grow, and a disruption in physical and mental development. When later cared for by emotionally involved and loving caretakers who give the babies an opportunity to form a loving relationship, these infants resume normal mental and physical development.

Everything you do with your baby contributes to the bonds of attachment. The following three activities offer you especially rich opportunities to enhance the bonding process.

TOUCHING

The parts of the brain that process tactile information are more developed at birth than those involved with vision or hearing. So it's touch that first gives infants a way to judge and react to their surroundings. Touch also gives infants an emotional sense of security and in this way becomes a most important component in the bonding process.

Although touching your baby is unavoidable in day-to-day caretaking, you can augment the bonding capabilities of touch by paying special attention to the frequency and sensitivity with which you touch. Take time to stroke your baby's skin while bathing and diapering. Learn more about the art of baby massage as a way of improving parenting skills, the baby's well-being, and the parent/infant relationship. (See the book about infant massage recommended at the end of this chapter.) And keep in mind that each baby is unique in the way she processes stimulation. Some will immediately cuddle and coo and obviously enjoy being handled and stroked; others will stiffen and arch their backs and show other signs of being a noncuddler. Experimentation and practice will help you find when and how you can touch your baby in ways that will make you both feel comfortable and "attached."

CARRYING

It won't take long for you to discover how much your new baby loves to be held. Although some well-meaning friends will warn you not to hold your infant too much for fear of spoiling him, don't listen. Before the age of six months, babies cannot be spoiled.

Infants cry to be held because their insecurities and fears are eased by the comfort of close physical contact. The time a baby spends cradled in your arms or lying against your body are times of bonding. To increase your opportunities for physical contact, you might put your baby in a body sling that holds the child against your body yet leaves your arms free to do other things. A recent study compared the developing relationship between mothers who kept their babies nearby but in infant seats and mothers who carried their babies in these soft baby carriers. The study documented that physical contact promoted by carrying does result in greater maternal responsiveness and more secure attachment between infant and mother.[1]

PLAYING

It is well known that pleasurable relationships can create deeply satisfying attachments. Even infants enjoy the fun of playing games and watching you smile, giggle, and change expression and tone of voice. The importance of playing with your baby is detailed in Mistake #16 and a sampling of language games is offered in Mistake #11. Playing with infants is a means of establishing an enjoyable parent/child relationship that is easily continued on into childhood long after your baby can no longer be carried around or easily held still long enough for a massage.

Bonding opportunities are endless. For parents of "easy," smiling babies the process generally runs smoothly and quite naturally. Parents of babies who suffer bouts of colic or who have difficult temperaments will find, however, that it may take some daily effort to smile, coo, and hold lovingly this child who wants to do little more than scream. Because your attitude toward your baby is such a vital element in the bonding process, it is important to find ways to enjoy your child. Every chapter of this book is written with that goal in mind; so as you read, consider how avoiding each mistake will help you find more pleasurable ways to bond with your baby.

Recommended for further reading:

Infant Massage: A Handbook for Loving Parents
Vimala Schneider McClure
Bantam, 1989

"Putting" Your Baby to Sleep

I t's 3:30 A.M. and six-month-old Jason is once again crying for his parents. "This is maddening," growls his dad. "When is this kid gonna sleep through the night?" "I don't know," sighs his wife, "but I do know it's your turn to give him his bottle." Jason's parents know that the feeding will put him to sleep, but after six months of night crying and feeding, they don't want to do it anymore. Unfortunately, the habit of "putting" Jason to sleep, which they fell into when Jason was a newborn, is now a tough one for Jason to break.

Most new parents expect to lose some sleep after the baby's arrival. However, what you may not expect or fully understand until you've had a few months of firsthand experience, is the wide range of physical and psychological consequences that sleep deprivation can cause. These problems, which include fatigue, irritability, anxiety, depression, anger, resentment, and guilt, certainly detract from the joy of loving a baby.

Although babies as young as four to eight weeks of age can be trained to sleep through the night, it is a mistake to try to remedy the sleepless-night problem by "putting" a baby to sleep. Putting to sleep is a bad habit that begins when parents find that their babies will drift off more easily under certain conditions. Some parents, for example, feed their babies or rock them until they doze off; others walk or pat the babies' backs until they snooze; and others play music, give a pacifier, or offer a ride in the carriage or car.

NIGHT CRIERS

These techniques of putting a baby to sleep usually *do* work. However, although they work and you may not mind practicing them during the day, you will find it maddening to do them at night.

All babies under one year of age wake during the night for short periods. Once awake, some lay quietly in bed and then fall back to sleep; others cry persistently until someone comes to soothe them. The babies who fall back to sleep are called self-soothers; they have learned how to put themselves to sleep without outside help. Those babies who cry out for their parents are called trained night criers; they have learned to need someone to rock, walk, feed, or nurse them to sleep. When these babies wake they need their parents to reestablish the outside sleep aids they've been conditioned to need. The goal of what can be called sleep training, then, is simply to help an infant fall asleep without parental help.

It's misleading to say that babies can be taught to sleep through the night because no one really does. As we go from one level of sleep to another, we all wake and fall back to sleep several times each night. Although babies sometimes cry out for a brief period as they pass from one stage to another, when left alone, they cry for a few minutes and then fall asleep. But when anxious parents rush in and pick up their babies and then feed or rock them, the babies' natural sleep patterns and processes are disturbed. Soon the babies lose their natural self-soothing abilities and begin the habit of night waking that will keep them (and their parents) from getting a good night's sleep for weeks or even months to come.

SLEEP TRAINING

Sleep training can begin when the baby is only three days old. To begin, parents should try to keep their infants from falling asleep while feeding or rocking, et cetera. If they do fall asleep, they should be woken, and then put into bed while still awake. You may think it's crazy to wake a baby so you can put her back to sleep, but each time you do, you give the baby an opportunity to practice self-soothing. You'll be glad you tried this "crazy" idea when your baby can fall asleep without your help in the middle of the night.

When you put your wide-awake baby into bed, he may cry at first. In fact, many babies soothe themselves, discharge tension, and relax by crying. If your baby wants to cry for a while before going to sleep (five to ten minutes of crying is common), let him do it (and then reread Mistake #4 about the positive aspects of crying!).

DARK-LIGHT CYCLE

You can encourage your baby to sleep (without your help) for longer periods during the night and shorter periods during the day by helping her set her internal clock to a dark-light cycle. You can do this right from the moment of birth by following these guidelines:

Daytime

• Keep your baby's room bright and well lit during the day. Even at nap time, keep the shades up and curtains open.

• Limit the length of daytime naps to three hours. Offer a feeding after the nap and then play with your baby to encourage wakefulness.

• Don't try to hush household noises when your baby is napping. Vacuum whenever you want; let siblings play, and don't keep the phone off the hook (unless *you* want to sleep). Babies need sleep and they'll learn to sleep under whatever conditions they are introduced to from the beginning.

Nighttime

• Try to keep your baby awake from 8 P.M. to 10 P.M. This will lessen the likelihood of falling asleep early but then waking several times before morning. Many parents find they can keep their babies awake longer by stimulating them with an early evening bath. Although babies between four and eight weeks old, who fall asleep at 9 P.M., may still wake for a midnight feeding (see "Focal Feeding" below), they should then be able to sleep until 5 A.M. Studies indicate that during this age period, babies can extend their longest sleep time from four to eight hours..

• Don't excite the baby or begin any kind of vigorous play in the hour before bedtime.

- When you put the baby to bed, keep the baby's room dark and quiet.
- If you feed the baby during the night, do it quietly. Don't turn on the light (a hall or night light will do); don't play with the baby; change the diaper only if absolutely necessary, and then promptly return the baby to the crib.

FOCAL FEEDING

A focal feeding between the hours of 10 P.M. and midnight helps babies stretch out the time between night feedings. Following the guidelines below, you can begin focal feedings when the baby is as young as three days old:

- Pick a convenient time between 10 P.M. and midnight when you will be consistently available to feed the baby.
- Wake the baby at this same time every night.
- Give a complete feeding. Try not to let the baby fall back to sleep during the feeding. This is difficult to do with newborns, but if you persist, the method will eventually work.
- Continue this focal feeding until your baby is three to five months old or weighs more than eleven pounds.

Remember that between four and eight weeks of age, many babies are physically able to stretch their sleep pattern to a full eight hours. This sounds like good news, but if you put your baby to bed for the night at 8 P.M., the eight-hour stretch ends too soon at 4 A.M. and so it certainly doesn't seem as if the baby is sleeping "through the night." By giving the last focal feeding at 11 P.M. you will help your baby sleep through to 7 A.M.—for most parents, this is certainly an easier schedule to live with.

STRETCH FEEDINGS

If your six-week-old baby who has been gaining weight and has reached nine or ten pounds is still not sleeping five to six consecutive hours each night, you may find nighttime relief by stretching out the daytime and nighttime feedings. The purpose of stretching is to break the baby's wake-up—expect-to-eat pattern that may be causing her to call for you during the night.

Daytime

When your baby wakes from a daytime nap, try this procedure:

• Change the baby's diaper. Do this slowly and deliberately to pass some time.

• Take the baby for a walk, rock in the rocking chair, dance around the floor, or play distracting games. Try to keep your baby occupied so he doesn't cry for a feeding.

• Don't hold the baby in the feeding position during this stretching time.

Delay the time between waking and feeding for as long as you can. You might be able to stretch the time for only ten minutes at first, but eventually you will be able to stretch the time to forty-five minutes. This change of schedule will discourage the association the baby has made between waking and feeding.

Nighttime

You can continue to stretch feedings at nighttime as well. Although a step-by-step process is fully explained in the book listed at the end of this chapter, you can successfully support your baby's efforts to learn how to sleep through the night by using focal feedings as explained earlier and by continuing to train your baby to fall asleep without your help.

A child's night-waking is a bad habit that can disturb a family's sleep for years. You'll find that teaching your baby now how to sleep soundly and independently is well worth the effort in the long run.

Recommended for further reading:

Helping Your Child Sleep Through the Night
Joanne Cuthbertson and Susie Schevill
Doubleday, 1985

Feeding to Soothe

J an fed and diapered her four-month-old before they went for a walk to the park. Once out in the fresh air, little Kelly was quite content to watch the other children going to and fro on the swings. But after a while, the scenery became monotonous and she began to squirm in her stroller; shortly, her boredom escalated into full-blown fury. Jan jiggled the stroller a bit and with her finger against her lips she whispered a "shhhhing" sound, but still Kelly screamed. Although Jan knew the baby couldn't really be hungry again so soon, she picked her up and offered her the bottle. After some initial resistance, Kelly began sucking and quieted down.

It's true that breast- or bottle-feeding will often stop an infant's cries, but it is not the food that calms the distress—it is the opportunity to suck. Many infants have strong sucking needs that are not fully met during feeding times. When offered the nipple between feedings, many will latch on as if starving, but in fact the baby does not want or need food, he simply wants to suck on the nipple or will accept it as a substitute for some other unmet need. When parents like Jan learn that the breast or bottle almost magically stops bouts of crying, it becomes understandably difficult to resist using food as a soothing technique (even when it's obvious the child is not hungry). Before you get into the habit of offering food to soothe, consider these negative effects that can result from the habit.

DISRUPTION OF THE NATURAL HUNGER CUES

Many babies are fed on demand. This method of feeding caters to the baby's individual needs and doesn't restrict the child's food intake to an arbitrary schedule. Although this is a positive and popular approach to feeding, parents are too easily convinced that every cry signals a "demand" for food. And so it is not uncommon for babies to have feedings every hour or even half-hour around the clock.

Once this kind of "snacking" schedule is established, babies have trouble learning to fill their stomachs in one feeding. They become accustomed to and begin to prefer small continuous feedings. Now the parents are stuck with a child who is constantly crying for the nipple and neither the baby nor the parents are quite sure if the cry comes from a need to be comforted through sucking or to be relieved from hunger. Although it's tiring for parents to keep up this relentless feeding schedule, it's the easiest way to stop the crying and so the cycle of cry-feed-cry-feed continues.

OVERFEEDING

Many parents worry that their infants aren't getting enough nourishment and so they offer food every time the child cries out. The fact is, more American babies are overfed than underfed. A contributing factor in overfeeding is precisely the use of breast or bottle to soothe distress.

You'll be better able to decide if your baby's cries are a sign of hunger when you learn to recognize her "hunger cry." As described in Mistake #4, the hunger cry is usually a rhythmic one that repeats a cry-pause-cry-pause pattern. The baby may also smack her lips or suck on fingers between cries. The easiest way to test a cry for hunger is to pick up your baby; if she stops crying, hunger isn't the problem.

MAKING THE WRONG CONNECTIONS

Infants possess very sensitive internal cues that signal when and how much they need to eat. Many research studies have monitored infants' innate ability to eat only enough to satisfy hunger and only as often as needed. However, eating habits are also strongly influenced by external experiences that can scramble internal cues. Feeding to soothe cries rather than ease hunger can change the association between hunger and food that infants come equipped to make. Soon babies learn that food can be used to soothe distress. This reverses the natural order of feel-hunger/cry-for-food and changes it to cry-from-boredom, -fear, -or -tiredness/get-food. As they get older these babies look to the bottle or breast for comfort when they feel tired or insecure. As grown children and adults they may continue this association between solace and eating, and find that they eat in response to stress rather than hunger.

STAYING ON THE RIGHT TRACK

There are a number of tactics you can use to avoid this feeding problem. First, ask your pediatrician to recommend an appropriate feeding schedule (even demand schedules are usually spaced at least two hours apart). Although each baby's feeding needs are unique, certainly no baby should require another feeding fifteen minutes after the last. In the first few months healthy babies are fed an average of seven to ten times a day. Knowing approximately when your baby should be hungry will help you resist offering a feeding every time he cries. If you continue to worry that your baby is undernourished, keep a careful record of weight gain. If the child is steadily gaining about an ounce a day (except for the first few weeks after birth when most babies lose a few ounces), he is getting enough to eat.

Second, before you reach for the bottle, try a variety of other soothing techniques. If your baby has strong sucking needs, a pacifier may make life much happier for both of you. If you find yourself with a crying baby and no pacifier, place your pinkie finger in your baby's mouth and let her suck. If the crying continues, try some of the soothing techniques described in Mistake #2. Maybe your baby is bored, tired, or needs to feel the comfort of your arms. None of these problems are best handled with a breast or bottle nipple.

If you know your baby isn't hungry, but she obviously wants to suck on a breast or bottle nipple, offer a water bottle. Water will not confuse the eating cycle and will not cause overfeeding, but it very well may stop the crying. If, at first, your baby rejects water, try buying bottled spring water if your tap water has an odd taste, or letting cold water warm to room temperature. If your doctor approves, you might also use water sweetened with fruit juice or sugar; a recent study that evaluated sources of calming in one- to three-day-old infants found that infants who were given a water and sucrose mixture cried much less than infants who sucked on a pacifier.[1]

As a general rule, when your baby is crying at a nonfeeding time, don't automatically reach for food. Because babies have many other needs that make them cry, first investigate what else you might do to comfort your baby.

Recommended for further reading:

Child of Mine: Feeding with Love and Good Sense
Ellyn Satter
Bull Publishing, 1983

Bringing Baby into Your Bed

Three years ago, Marie and Hank made room between them in their bed for their infant daughter. "This made it easy to nurse Ashley at night without even getting out of bed," remembers Marie. "Yeah," adds Hank, "it seemed like a good idea at the time, but now Ashley's still lying between us and it's not okay anymore. None of us has had a good night's sleep in three years." No matter how many times Marie puts her daughter into her own bed each night, Ashley finds her way back to the family bed.

Marie and Hank told me their story when they visited Fairleigh Dickinson University's clinic for children with sleep problems. This clinic is crowded with parents telling the same tale: "We can't get our child to sleep in his own room." Because this family-bed situation interferes with pleasurable child rearing for so many parents, I've learned to advise against it. But I also realize that there is no absolute right or wrong side to this issue. Certainly millions of well-adjusted and happy children in cultures around the world have been raised in family beds. The decision to bring an infant into your bed is an individual one that should be made after consideration of personal desires, needs, and beliefs. But certainly, because so many parents like Marie and Hank regret their decision, you should consider the following disadvantages of the family bed before you decide to let your infant sleep with you.

DISADVANTAGES OF THE FAMILY BED

The most obvious and frightening reason to keep an infant out of your bed is to avoid the danger of rolling over on the child, causing injury or death by suffocation. It has happened. Be especially wary if you or your spouse sleep soundly, use large fluffy pillows, or sleep on a very soft mattress or water bed; these factors increase the risk of unintentionally harming your baby.

The family bed should also be given a second thought if it will cause family tensions. If only one parent wants the child in the bed, for example, the marital problems that can grow from resentment, feelings of isolation, and lack of privacy can be much more difficult

to fix than the problem of a night-crying baby. Bringing your infant to bed may also upset an older sibling who's already struggling with feelings of neglect. Although I know some parents welcome all their children into their bed, I've heard personally only from those who would give a king's ransom to get their children back into their own beds.

Nursing mothers, like Marie, often like the idea of having the baby close during the night, but it's in-bed nursing that causes many of the difficulties that will eventually grow from this habit of bringing the baby to your bed. Nursing (or bottle feeding, for that matter) while lying down is discouraged by pediatricians because they have noted a connection between feeding a baby who's lying in a horizontal position and chronic ear infections. Parents are advised to tilt the baby's body to a more upright position so the fluid does not pool in the immature ear canal. Check with your pediatrician before you decide to feed the baby while either of you is lying down. Additionally, babies who are able to nurse continually during the night are not always willing to give up their "snacking" schedule during the day. Many mothers find it impossible to satisfy a nursing infant who has learned to use nursing as a soothing device. As explained in Mistakes #7 and #9, feeding to soothe causes many problems of its own, and being denied the opportunity to become a self-soother affects the child's ultimate ability to separate from the parents. In our society, which relies heavily on day-care, babysitters, and preschool, children need to be able to calm and comfort themselves at an early age. Needing a parent's physical closeness to feel secure or to fall asleep has obvious disadvantages for the child.

The family bed can also negatively affect children if the sleeping arrangements keep their mothers from getting a good night's sleep and contribute to the fatigue of being on duty twenty-four hours a day. Initially, bringing an infant to bed may seem like a solution to the tiredness caused by answering night cries, but as discussed in Mistake #6, the first few months (or even only weeks) of night crying and night feeding end much sooner for the parents who schedule night feedings and let their babies sleep in a separate room than for those who offer continuous night feedings in bed and later find that the baby won't sleep alone.

Some parents don't mind sharing their beds for an indefinite period of time; others do. If you like the idea of snuggling with your infant, but would balk at the intrusion of a four-year-old who flails, tosses, turns, and kicks, you'd better think twice before letting your infant settle in. Infant sleep problems like crying and wakefulness don't always disappear by themselves. A study of children with sleep problems at eight months found that 41 percent still had a problem at three years.[1] That's a lot of sleepless nights for a lot of people. It makes sense to me to deal with the night crying problem early on to ensure that your baby will develop healthy sleep habits in the years to come.

Keeping your baby out of your bed has nothing to do with good or bad parenting. It's a personal decision of preference. But when you make that decision, remember that there is nothing "cruel" about setting a night/day pattern that clearly establishes that daytime is for cuddling, playing, and loving and nighttime is for sleeping. There's also nothing that says once you decide to keep your baby in the nursery you can't occasionally break that rule. During thunderstorms, for example, or in times of stress or illness, you might choose to comfort your child by keeping her in your bed. But a word to the wise says: If you don't want family sleeping to become a habit, don't let the exception stretch to even two nights. In a child's mind, two nights in a row sets a new standard of routine. Far better, in the long run, to go to your child's room. Offer comfort with words and touch. Stay nearby, stroke the hair, sing a lullaby, or even spend the night there if necessary. But keep your children in their beds so they learn to accept their own rooms as enjoyable, secure places.

Discouraging "Lovies"

I 'm not going to make the same mistake with this baby that I did with her brother and sister," Sue assured her husband. "There's no way Jenny is going to get attached to a blanket like David did or a doll like Melissa did, even if I have to rotate toys and blanket every day."

Sue feels strongly about this subject of "lovies," as they're sometimes called, because for her, the blanket and doll were a constant source of embarrassment and inconvenience. When David went to preschool at age three, he screamed for his dirty and tattered blanket. And because Melissa refused to go to sleep without her doll, more often than not her parents spent the early evening hours searching the house, scouting the backyard with flashlights, and calling neighbors and friends trying to find Melissa's lost "Dolly." From her point of view, Sue has good reason to discourage her new baby's attachment to a lovie, but from the baby's view, it's a mistake.

By eight or nine months of age, many babies begin to cling to their blankets, pacifiers, stuffed animals, dolls, fingers, or thumbs. These sources of comfort have been labeled "transitional objects" because they give children something to depend upon as they begin to reach for independence. Toddlers want to venture out on their own, but because they're unsure of exactly what's out there, some need someone or something to cling to for support as they give independence a try. Although most parents try to give their babies the assurances they need during this developmental stage, there are times when even the most caring moms and dads can't be there—bedtime, nursery school time, and babysitter time, for example. Transitional objects are used as adaptive mechanisms that help children soothe themselves as they learn to become more independent and cope with stress on their own.

Although lovies can be annoying to parents, the problems they cause are generally small in comparison to the benefits they offer. Some parents worry that the need for a comforting object is a sign of an insecure personality. Research assures us, however, that this is just not so. In a recent study, 108 children ages twenty months to four years were rated on their attachment to blankets and on how much they feared separation, dogs, storms, and a variety of social events. When the results were tabulated, researchers found that blanket-attached children were neither more nor less secure than unattached children.[1]

Similarly, some parents discourage thumb-sucking because they worry it will cause protruding teeth. Although it's true that many babies who learn in infancy to soothe themselves by sucking on their fingers or thumbs continue the habit into the preschool years, the vast majority of children stop thumb-sucking before their permanent teeth come in. If a child still thumb-sucks when permanent teeth start to emerge, there are effective remedies that parents can use at that time to stop the habit, as explained in the book *How to Help Children with Common Problems* by C. E. Schaefer and H. Millman (Plume, 1981).

Yet other parents are mortified by the way their babies look with pacifiers in their mouths. In infancy, babies often need pacifiers to satisfy an instinctive need for sucking. Although this need begins to diminish at six months of age, long after this time some babies still find comfort in sucking. Although it annoys and embarrasses their parents, some will continue to want their pacifier well into the preschool years. And still other parents whose babies choose blankets or dolls for their comfort objects worry that these dirty, torn, threadbare, saliva-matted "things" are outright health hazards.

These problems are common to this growing stage. Some children cling to their transitional objects with greater urgency and for longer periods than others. But by age five, most children gradually put aside their lovies willingly and without fanfare. Although some may continue to seek their comforting objects at nighttime or in times of stress or illness, even into their teens, experts agree that in most cases the attachment still isn't anything to worry about unless the child begins to withdraw from normal social interactions to be with the object. At that point, the child may be showing signs of needing a more nurturing and stimulating environment. But as the majority of children become more secure with their position in the world, they'll soon be ready to venture out alone without a lovie.

Knowing how transitional objects help toddlers comfort themselves, you can encourage object attachment while your children are still infants. You might use the same blanket in the crib each day, cuddle them always with the same stuffed animal or doll, or rock them with the same cloth over your shoulder. Consistently offering the same item while you're holding and loving your babies will encourage them to associate that object with you.

If your children become attached to comforting items, don't worry about what they'll look like clinging to their lovies as they get older; give them what they need to feel secure and comforted now. Then use the following tips, which can make it a bit easier for you to get through this transitional stage:

• If you notice in infancy that your baby seems particularly soothed by a specific object, buy three or four more! Toddlers are ferociously reluctant to accept a new lovie when their favorite is lost, ripped, or dirtied. If, however, they have several equally loved and worn objects, they will often take the switch in stride.

• Do not use a bottle as a comfort item. Mistake #7 explains fully why food should never be used as a soothing device.

• Some parents have successfully lured their child's blanket away long enough to cut it into several pieces. In this way they can launder a piece at a time, and place one piece at Grandma's, one at the babysitter's, and one at home.

• After the age of two years, you can begin to wean your child from the public use of the lovie. With increasing frequency, leave it at home when you take a walk or a trip to the park. At home, don't leave it always visible; instead, put it aside and wait for your child to ask for it. Gradually, you can introduce rules that say the lovie must stay home. You'll have to see how your child reacts before you make it a hard and fast rule, however. Some accept the idea graciously; others scream unmercifully.

In the end, remember: Although you may feel embarrassed or inconvenienced by transitional objects, they help your child feel secure and that's what really matters.

Misreading Your Baby's Temperament

As Hank tried to get his three-month-old son into the car, Joey pulled his usual "I-hate-my-car-seat" routine by arching his back, flailing his arms, and screaming in protest. "I can't stand taking this kid anywhere," Hank admitted to his wife. "Especially to family gatherings like this one. It's so aggravating to watch everyone swoon over my brother's 'darling' baby while ours does nothing but cry. Then my mother will start her lecture about all the things we're doing wrong. Although I know we'll end up arguing, I think she's right; we must be doing something wrong. Why do you think little Kate just sits around and smiles at everybody, while Joey screams and kicks and carries on the whole time we're there?"

"I don't know," sighed Hank's wife, Denise, who has wondered the same thing many times. "Maybe he's just naturally crabby."

Denise's offhand remark is actually not far from the truth. There is evidence that infants do possess distinct temperaments that dictate the way they react to their parents, to other people, and to their environment. In the 1950s, child development researchers Alexander Thomas and Stella Chess began a now famous thirty-year longitudinal study out of New York University Medical Center. They followed 133 infants from birth to adulthood and found that children do come equipped with their own unique personalities.[1] Today, prominent child rearing authorities agree and find that the most successful and satisfied parents are those who can adjust their parenting strategies to complement their child's temperament.

Thomas and Chess established nine categories of temperamental characteristics that make babies differ from each other. It seems likely these characteristics are inherited, and as a new parent you need to know they exist so you do not mistakenly take sole credit for an "easy" infant, nor, like Hank, take complete blame for a "difficult" one. (Interestingly, these differences seem to have little relationship to the child's sex or birth order.)

The nine behavioral characteristics used by Thomas and Chess to identify temperament are: 1. activity level; 2. regularity of biological functions such as sleeping and eating; 3. adaptability, or the length of time it takes for the child to adapt to new situations; 4. approach or withdrawal when faced with a new person or situation; 5. threshold of sensitivity, which indicates the intensity of stimuli necessary to bring about a response; 6. the intensity of reaction, or the energy level of the child's response; 7. distractibility, which notes how easily a child can be pulled away from an activity; 8. quality of mood, which determines if the child is generally joyful or sad; and 9. attention span or persistence, which measures a child's eagerness to return to a task if interrupted.

These behavioral characteristics are not necessarily permanent or unchanging, but they are certainly present at birth in identifiable patterns that often continue into early adulthood. For example, in the Thomas-Chess study (and in today's infant population as well) approximately 40 percent of the children were "easy," 10 percent were "difficult," 15 percent were "slow to warm up," and the remainder showed combinations of temperament traits that did not fit neatly into one of these three categories. The "easy," "difficult," and "slow to warm up" labels are still used to identify infant temperaments.

What kind of baby do you have? Put a check next to the question responses below that most accurately describe your child's behavior *most* of the time.

1. ACTIVITY
When you change your baby's diaper, does she:
___ a. lie quietly
___ b. kick and cry most of the time
___ c. wiggle and squirm

2. REGULARITY

Between midnight and 5 A.M. is your baby:

✓ a. asleep
__ b. awake three times or more
__ c. awake once or twice

3. ADAPTABILITY

When you take your baby to the supermarket does he:

✓ a. enjoy the trip and seem interested in the changing environment
__ b. cry inconsolably until you return home
__ c. cry when you first enter the store but then calm down with only occasional whimpers of complaint

4. APPROACH

When a stranger comes toward your baby does she:

✓ a. smile and reach toward the person
__ b. pull away and scream until the stranger leaves
__ c. fuss and shy away

5. SENSITIVITY

If the telephone rings while your baby is sleeping will he most likely:

✓ a. sleep through the noise
__ b. awaken instantly
__ c. whimper or cry out but then fall back to sleep

6. INTENSITY

When your baby is hungry does she:

__ a. make sucking noises or suck her fingers without much complaining
✓ b. scream frantically before you have a chance to offer food
✓ c. cry on and off until you offer food

7. DISTRACTIBILITY

If someone walks into the room while you're feeding your baby, does he:

__ a. continue feeding
✓ b. stop and turn toward the noise
__ c. slow the sucking pace then continue feeding

8. MOOD

During the course of a day, does your baby spend most of her awake time:

__ a. pleasantly

__ b. crying

__ c. showing no particular pattern

9. ATTENTION SPAN

When your baby watches something over the crib, does he:

__ a. watch intently for an extended period

__ b. turn away looking for something else after only a few seconds

__ c. seem quite variable in attention

To find out your baby's dominant characteristics, add up how many checks you have next to "a" responses, how many next to "b," and how many next to "c."

If you have placed five or more checks next to a's, your baby can be called an "easy" baby. These babies generally follow regular schedules, have a positive approach to change, and experience mild mood swings. "Easy" babies obviously make life more pleasant for their parents, but they can be a source of worry as well. Despite their pediatricians' assurances, some parents become unduly alarmed that babies who are slow to respond and who are quiet and inactive may be suffering some degree of retardation or other neurological abnormality. Knowing about these temperamental characteristics should help you accept and enjoy your baby's delightful personality.

If you have five or more checks next to b's, your baby may have a "difficult" temperament. While no specific set of traits makes babies difficult, some possess certain combinations of traits that certainly make them much harder to care for. These include: irregularity, withdrawal, negative moods, and intense reactions. If you have a difficult baby, you already know that raising these children can be very stressful. You also need to realize that the trying times caused by your baby's inborn personality are not caused by your lack of parenting skills. To love and nurture this kind of baby, you will need a great deal of patience, as well as an abundance of child rearing tactics that use approval and affection when the child is comfortable and cooperative. You will also need more time away from your baby and some supportive help from your spouse and family so you can recharge the physical and emotional strength you need to meet the demands on your time and energy.

If you have five or more checks next to "c" responses, your baby may have a combination of personality traits that place him in a category called "slow to warm up." These babies tend to display mildly negative responses to new stimuli. They are cautious and need to approach strangers and new situations slowly, at their own pace.

If the majority of your check marks don't fall in any pattern, your baby probably has temperamental traits that are a mixture of the three most easily recognized patterns.

The advantage in knowing about your child's temperament is not in getting the child to change to fit your expectations; it is, instead, in having an opportunity to create a good fit between your temperament and your child's. Recognizing that some behaviors are based on inborn personality characteristics can help you be more sympathetic to your child, respond more objectively to her needs and demands, and, so very important, not blame yourself or consider the child "abnormal" if she is difficult to handle. You can best encourage your child to grow in confidence and self-esteem by finding and focusing on the pleasurable aspects of your child's oh-so-very individual temperament.

Recommended for further reading:

The Difficult Child
Stanley Turecki and Leslie Tonner
Bantam, 1985

Pooh-poohing Baby Talk

"C oochey, coochey, coo! Oh, wittle bitty baby is soooo pwitty and Mommy wuvs him so so so so much! Does wittle bitty baby wuv his mommy too?"

This kind of incessant baby babbling is more than Andrea's friends can stand for any length of time. "Everytime she looks at the baby, her voice raises five octaves," says her sister, who's tired of the goo-goo conversations. "She talks in this annoying singsong way even though I keep telling her that baby talk is bad for the baby."

Andrea has listened to her sister's warning about the dangers of baby talk, but still she changes her usual conversational style and tone when she talks to her baby. "I know I sound ridiculous," Andrea says, "but it just feels right and I really think my two-month-old listens to me more when I talk that way."

How, when, and even if we should baby-talk to our infants is often a point of debate among new parents. No matter which philosophy is in vogue at the time you deliver your baby, the fact is that some form of baby talk is used in every culture that has ever been studied—certainly clear evidence of its intrinsic value. Don't worry about how "silly" you may sound; use the following guidelines to find a comfortable blend of baby and adult talk that will encourage your baby to learn the fun and practical use of our language.

BABY TALK

Andrea has gone over the line of constructive language encouragement by mispronouncing words like *love* and *little* and translating them into the babiese words *wuv* and *wittle*. But if she combines proper word pronunciation with her other baby talk strategies, she'll be using a technique that has been shown to foster language development in children. When you talk to your baby remember these guidelines:

• Try to eliminate background noise like the TV or radio. It's difficult for an infant to concentrate on your voice when there are other sounds to listen to.

• Use a higher than usual pitch in a singsong manner. Studies indicate that high-pitched sounds attract an infant's attention and melodic intonation keeps that attention longer than normal adult conversational tone. In fact, researchers now suspect that this "infant-directed speech" is preferred over adult speech patterns by babies as young as two days old.[1]

• Speak slowly, and use simple words and short sentences. In casual conversation, many adults tend to slur words and ramble one sentence into the next. Speaking clearly and simply will help your baby become accustomed to the sounds of specific words and basic sentence structures.

• Engage your baby's interest in conversation by keeping your face about twelve inches from hers, by using an animated style, and by changing your facial expressions.

• When you talk to your baby, pause occasionally as if waiting for a response. Ask questions and allow a few moments of silence to pass before continuing the conversation. As early as one month of age, you may be surprised to hear a cooing response.

• Although you should talk to your baby all day long, schedule "conversations" with newborns when they're in quiet states of alertness with eyes bright and focused. As they get a bit older, conversations are most enjoyable when babies are rested, fed, and changed.

Some parents feel awkward talking to a little person who doesn't talk back. Although it's true that infants don't yet make the best conversationalists, they do enjoy and learn from conversational-type chatter. Don't talk just for the sake of talking; talk *with* your baby. Ask questions; pause for answer time. Loosen up; laugh, joke, enjoy. You probably won't find such an eager listener again. Don't make the mistake of shying away from baby talk. It's a wonderful way to entertain, educate, and love your child.

LANGUAGE GROWTH

As in most other areas of development, babies learn language at different rates and in different ways. Some coo pleasantly; others grunt and squeak. Some babble incessantly; others listen intently. Some say their first word at seven months; others wait until well into their second or third year. And even then, language development doesn't follow a linear path; children tend to take two steps forward and then one step back. They forget words they once knew so well. Sometimes, they stop talking altogether for a while. And the proper use of words like *run* and *went* can suddenly become *runned* and *goed.* As you help your baby learn our language, have patience and above all put fun above progress. Don't let an emphasis on how soon or how well your child talks turn language development into a race or a chore.

The following chart is included in this chapter to give you an *idea* of what you can expect from your baby and how you can foster language at each stage. But remember: **These are only guidelines because no one can predict how your baby will progress through each stage.**

STAGES OF LANGUAGE DEVELOPMENT

Birth	Listens to speech. Vocalizes by crying. Enjoys listening to music and your singing.
Up to 2 Months	Coos pleasantly. Makes mostly vowel sounds. Will initiate communication, repeat sounds, and respond when given the opportunity.
3 Months	Enjoys action games and songs with repeated sequence of words like "Pat-a-Cake," "Row Row Row Your Boat," and "Ring Around the Rosey."
Up to 6 Months	Makes speechlike babbling sounds. Can make consonant sounds and may string together word sounds like "dadadadadadada."
Up to 9 Months	Begins to imitate sounds you make. May begin "talking" to get attention. Makes consonant vowel combinations (gu, ba, mo). Laughs out loud. Makes loud and soft sounds.

Up to 12 Months   Recognizes words for some objects. May say
                     several words like *Mama* and *bye-bye* and
                     repeat them over and over. Will "talk" with
                     inflection and expression. Listens when
                     spoken to and understands many words; if
                     asked, "Where's Mommy?" will point or look
                     in her direction.

Language development is a natural and inevitable occurrence,
but it does not happen equally in all children. One study of upper-
and middle-class children found that those whose parents re-
sponded to their gurgles and gestures talked more and had higher
IQs than children of less attentive parents.[2] This is not at all
surprising because it is well known that a strong foundation in
language is critical to social, emotional, and intellectual development. Don't let the sound of "baby talk" scare you away from such a
marvelous opportunity.

Recommended for further reading:

Language Games to Play with Your Baby
Allyssa McCabe
Fawcett Columbine, 1987

Delaying Separation

W hy don't you and Ted go out to dinner tonight?" asked Gloria's mother. "I'll watch the baby." Gloria's mom had made this offer many times before and so she knew her daughter's response would be an automatic "No." But this time she persisted. "What's the matter with you? Johnny's four months old and you've never once left him. Nothing will happen to him if you go out for just an hour or two—I think you both could use the break from each other."

"Don't start again," Gloria yelled over her shoulder as she left the room to get Johnny from his crib. "Johnny's got a runny nose and it might make him fussy tonight. I'm not going to leave him when he's sick."

"For one hour," pleaded her mom.

"No," repeated Gloria.

Many new moms (more often than dads) feel apprehensive about leaving their infants, and so they resist the idea of going anywhere without the baby. As desirable as a close parent/infant relationship is, moms like Gloria are setting themselves and their babies up for a difficult bout of separation anxiety when the child must eventually be left with someone other than the mother.

WHAT IS SEPARATION ANXIETY?

Separation anxiety can be defined as the emotional distress a child feels when shut off from her parents for any length of time. Normal children experience separation anxiety in varying degrees as a developmental stage in two parts. As early as three months (and peaking between six and nine months) infants show signs of stranger anxiety. As babies learn to distinguish themselves from others, they may cry at the sight of unfamiliar faces, and they may reject people who look different than their parents—eyeglasses or a beard will send some babies into hysterics. When this happens and a baby cries at the sight of a babysitter, for example, a parent's natural reaction may be to stop leaving the baby with the sitter. But, in fact, to better prepare for the period of separation anxiety that will follow sometime between six and twelve months of age, parents should use this time in infancy to rehearse separation.

PREPARING THE BABY FOR SEPARATION

All mentally healthy children will go through a period of separation anxiety. You can lessen the trauma of this anxious period, however, by taking some preparatory steps while your child is still in infancy.

Once your baby is one month old, create regular opportunities for separation. Call upon willing relatives; find a reliable sitter; or trade sitting time with another mother so you can leave your baby at least once a week for one- to two-hour periods. This will establish a comfortable routine for your baby and will also give you time to schedule weekly dates with your spouse, or do something else just for yourself. Starting this routine soon after birth has advantages because your baby won't yet protest being left behind, and setting up regular separation time will help both you and the baby continue the schedule when the baby gets old enough to complain about your absence.

Separation "games" can help your baby understand that when you leave, you also come back. When your baby is awake and alert, leave the room for a brief period of time, but maintain voice contact. Then return directly to the baby with a playful tickle or cuddle. Over time, leave the room for increasingly longer periods to teach your baby that just because you're out of sight doesn't mean you've disappeared. Peek-a-boo and hide-and-seek are also playful ways to teach the reassuring reality of object permanence.

When you plan to depart, hold your baby and engage in a brief period of upbeat, smiling conversation with the babysitter. Some child experts feel that there can be a transfer of positive feelings from the parent to the child toward the caretaker. Show your baby that you feel good about this person.

As your child gets older and shows increasing dismay at times of separation, try always to use babysitters who are familiar to your baby. If you hire someone new, allow plenty of getting-acquainted time before you leave.

PREPARING YOURSELF FOR SEPARATION

Some parents have more trouble than others separating from their babies. Parents who are highly anxious about separation find themselves in agreement with statements such as:

• When I am away from my child, I feel lonely and miss her a great deal.

• I am much better at keeping my child safe than any other person.

• I believe that my child misses me a great deal when I have to let someone else take care of him for a while.

If you find yourself feeling guilty or apprehensive at the thought of leaving your infant, you can ease your own separation anxiety by following these guidelines:

Find a capable sitter. Family members are most desirable sitters, but sometimes they are not available on a regular basis and so you may need to find a competent, caring person you can count on. The more confidence you have in your sitter, the less worried you'll feel while you're gone.

Never sneak out. It's easier and faster to duck out the door when the baby isn't looking, but it defeats the goal of easing separation anxiety. It's confusing and upsetting, even to an infant, to suddenly realize that you're not around and have no idea where you are or if you'll be back. Make it part of your good-bye routine to talk to your sitter and to your baby before you leave. Let your baby see you depart and later see you come back. It won't take long before she is able to realize that leaving is not a forever thing.

Stay calm. Emotions are contagious. Mothers who appear worried about separation pass this feeling on to their children. Don't prolong your good-byes by rushing back for another kiss; don't spend too much time sharing your forlorn expression and sorrowful tone of voice. Say good-bye cheerfully and then leave.

Although you can't eliminate the separation anxiety stage from your child's developmental calendar, early separation experiences can ease the upset of this trying time. They can also teach babies a valuable lesson: When Mom and Dad leave, babies can trust other adults until they return—and they always do return.

Recommended for further reading:

Oneness and Separateness: From Infant to Individual
Louise Kaplan
Simon & Schuster, 1980

Fueling Marital Tensions

T om wasn't looking for trouble when he arrived home, but he found it when he asked his wife, "Did you iron my blue shirt today?"

"Oh, gee," Pat shot back sarcastically. "While I was sitting around here watching TV and eating bon-bons all day, I could have done that for you. Sorry!" Then she began to sob. "You don't know what it's like being with this baby day in and day out. I'm tired and lonely and overwhelmed and all you care about is your shirt. Well, I've had it with your insensitivity and your macho attitude. Jason is your baby too, so you take care of him for a while."

"Give me a break," yelled Tom as he headed back out the door. "You think I'm having fun working overtime so you can stay home and complain?"

Although it may not sound like it, Tom and Pat do love each other and are both very happy about the birth of their son. Unfortunately, they've made the mistake of letting the conflicts of this readjustment period pull them in opposite directions.

CAUSES OF TENSION

Innumerable studies have documented that marital tensions and a decline in marital satisfaction very often accompany a baby's arrival as the new mom and dad both rapidly attempt to reorganize their lives. Along with excitement and joy, the majority of parents also experience unexpected emotions that jump around among feelings like anger, guilt, inadequacy, confinement, exhaustion, and isolation. These feelings can be especially difficult to handle because although men and women may react with equal intensity to the upheaval in their lives, they focus on very different aspects, making themselves emotionally inaccessible to each other.

Although there are many reasons for the marital problems that develop at this time, many new parents find common ground in their feelings of uncertainty and resentment, and in having sexual difficulties. If you find that you, too, are experiencing tension from any of these three areas, the following sections will assure you that you're not alone on the postbaby roller coaster ride and that if you pay attention to your marriage *before* trouble starts, you'll be able to lessen the stress and increase the bliss of having a new baby.

Uncertainty

WOMEN: As a new mother, you may feel uncertain about many things. Even experienced mothers can become unnerved because they don't always know how best to take care of their babies. Should they pick up an inconsolable crier? Should they begin solid foods when their infants seem hungry? Should they call the doctor about a low-grade fever? Rest assured that no one has all the right answers all the time; most new mothers struggle with feelings of inadequacy sooner or later.

MEN: As men become more vocal about their postbaby concerns, feelings of uncertainty clamor to the top of the list. It can be tough to find a comfortable balance between being the responsible provider, the sensitive husband, and the involved father. In fact, it's not uncommon for new dads to avoid facing their conflicting roles by finding reasons to stay away from home. Some become overly involved in community affairs; others find a renewed interest in athletics, and the largest number take on overtime projects at work. But the time away from home doesn't resolve the problem; it inflames it. Your wife may feel angry and abandoned, and you may feel more confused and pressured by yet another demand. Feelings of uncertainty are normal, but as with most problems, they won't go away until they are recognized and dealt with.

Resentment

WOMEN: Without a doubt, having a baby pushes parents into the battle that rages to answer the question "Who does more work in this family?" If you think your husband doesn't carry a fair load in the child rearing and housework departments, you're not alone and you're probably not wrong. A poll published in a recent issue of *Working Mother* found that 69 percent of men and 86 percent of women agree that even if a father supports the family financially, he should also do household chores or child rearing.[1] However, despite this theoretical agreement between men and women, another nationwide study found that fathers spend only about two and a half hours a week with their young children, and take on less than one-third of the child-care responsibilities. These numbers hold strong even in families in which the mother has a full-time job.[2] The gap between what should be and what is can easily lead to feelings of resentment.

Many new mothers also resent their husband's "freedom." In families where the mom stays home and the dad goes to work, it can be very aggravating for the woman to watch her husband walk out of the house every day into the world of adult conversations, "important" interactions, and financial rewards. She, on the other hand, often stays behind isolated from adult company to deal with a seemingly endless cycle of crying, feeding, diaper changing, and washing. Despite the fact that at-home parenting may have been a coveted choice, its daily reality makes many women seethe at the sound of a husband's cheerful query, "So, how was your day?"

Also, women who return to work often resent fighting logistical battles such as: Who brings the baby to child care? Who stays home when she's sick? Who takes time off for doctor visits? The answers to questions like these can imply whose job is more important. When the burden of responsibility seems to fall continually on the mother, resentment is likely to interfere with a peaceful marriage.

MEN: If you're like millions of new dads before you, you may resent your wife's preoccupation with the baby. As the infant gains a monopoly on her time and attentions, you may find yourself feeling jealous and emotionally excluded—this is quite natural.

Before the baby, your wife may have looked to you for advice; now she may imply through her possessive actions and attitudes that you can't do anything right for the baby. You may also wonder if fathering has any rewards at all when family and friends gush and rave over the mother and child and act as if you're not in the room. Most dads don't like to admit it, but it's difficult not to resent their wives, the babies, and the entire change of attitude that often accompanies parenthood.

Sexual Difficulties

WOMEN: Obstetricians often tell new parents that they can resume sexual intercourse six weeks after the baby is born. Initially, this may sound like good news, but unfortunately for many women, their bodies and psyches don't know about this arbitrary date and aren't ready at the six-week mark.

For purely physical reasons, some new mothers aren't anxious to resume sexual relations. Lingering pain or discomfort due to an espisiotomy, Caesarean incision, tender breasts, or lack of vaginal lubrication can make intercourse at this time very uncomfortable.

There are also an array of psychological reasons why you might need more time to fall back into your role as wife and lover. For one, sexual desire may be hard to muster if you feel overweight and worn-out. You may also be so mentally distracted that you worry you hear the baby crying every time your husband feels amorous. And not surprisingly, after being so physically involved with the baby all day, it would be quite normal if you didn't want one more person to touch you; you probably would rather retreat to your bed to snatch a few much-needed moments of sleep. With all these physical and psychological factors working against sexual desire, many women need more than six weeks to switch from their role as mother back to their role as lover.

MEN: As a new dad, you obviously don't have physical reasons that delay your return to sexual intimacy, but still you may not be ready to resume lovemaking. Many men hesitate because they worry that intercourse may hurt their wives or that it will feel different. Some find themselves less attracted to wives who are "out of shape" or who now represent mother figures rather than lovers. Others, who have none of these concerns, find energy and time limitations, as well as their wife's preoccupation with mothering, enormous obstacles to reestablishing the prebaby relationship.

When only one partner experiences sexual difficulties after the birth of a baby, resentment is likely to cause obvious marital tensions. When both partners are having difficulty relighting the fire, their mutual lack of interest can cause subtle tensions that grow from the worry that their love life will never be the way it was before the baby.

CURES FOR TENSIONS

Although some degree of marital tension is inevitable after the birth of a baby, it doesn't have to permanently damage your relationship. Learning to schedule your time and to talk about your feelings will assure that a postbaby decline in marital satisfaction does not become more than the temporary period of readjustment that it really is.

Make Time

To keep the tensions of resentment, fatigue, and uncertainty from boiling over, be sure to make time every week to do something just for *you.* Some smart mothers call on grandparents or babysitters so they can take a relaxing bath or shower without interruption. Others use relief time to take a walk, visit a friend, or sit in a locked room with a cup of coffee and the daily paper. Dads, too, need time to be free of responsibilities. Although, at first, this may feel self-indulgent, you both owe it to your marriage to get away from it for a short while every week.

Just as surely as you make time for your baby and yourself, *schedule time for your spouse.* Spontaneous moments of hand holding and eye gazing may have to be put on hold for a while, but there's no reason to totally put the person you love on hold. It's easy to become preoccupied with your new role as parent and/or breadwinner, so before tensions erupt, new parents have to promise each other at least fifteen minutes a day of undivided attention.

This time doesn't have to lead to sexual intimacy—just be together. When the baby goes to sleep (and all babies do at some time), turn off the TV, set aside the chores, and spend time with each other.

Talk

The most important point to remember about the roots of tension discussed in this chapter is that they are very commonly experienced by new parents. Unfortunately, in an attempt to appear confident and assured, many husbands and wives hide their unhappiness from each other. Don't make this mistake. Talk openly about how you feel and you may find that you both have ambivalent emotions that are difficult to deal with alone. Recognizing that you're both in the same situation will often help you get through this period of readjustment. Also, be sure to leave time for daily conversations that don't focus on the baby. Talk about outside interests, the before-baby days, and other family members and friends. Most important—keep talking to each other.

You'll also find it useful to talk with other parents. Nothing is more comforting and more apt to put your experiences in perspective than hearing another parent say, "I feel that way too!" Seek out the company of other parents and in your casual conversations you'll find helpful support.

The biggest mistake you can make in dealing with marital tensions is to choose this time to judge the worth of your entire marriage. Frazzled nerves and lack of sleep wreak havoc with anyone's coping mechanisms. As a new parent, you especially need to be extremely forgiving of yourself and your spouse at this time.

Recommended for further reading:

How to Stay Lovers While Raising Your Children
Ann Mayer
Price, Stern, Sloan, 1990

Trying to Be a "Perfect" Parent

I can't believe one baby can take up so much of my time and energy," Karen confided to her neighbor. "Before Brittany was born, I taught twenty-seven fifth graders every day, supervised an afterschool club, worked out at the spa, kept a clean home, and cooked Tom a good meal every night. Now, if I manage to brush my teeth and comb my hair by the time he gets home, I have to call it a good day. I can't figure out what I'm doing wrong."

Karen's experiences are common to many new parents; it's how she reacts to them, however, that will dramatically affect her emotional and physical health and therefore her ability to be a good parent. She may decide she wants to be a "perfect parent" and therefore steadfastly pursue a regimen that will put her back on her prebaby schedule. Or she may adjust her daily activities and reduce her expectations in the hope of being a merely "good" parent.

Although striving to be a perfect parent may seem to be the better choice, it is, unfortunately, an impossible goal to achieve. No one in any life situation can be all-knowing, all-giving, all-self-sacrificing, all-nurturing, all-accomplished, and all-loving all the time. Yet, so many new parents believe that to be a good parent they must be a perfect one. This misguided belief usually arises out of these three myths of parenthood:

MYTH #1
GOOD PARENTS DO IT ALL

Before the baby's arrival, couples can usually live rather neatly sched-
uled lives. They have clean clothes, three meals a day, an orderly
house, and delegated time for work, play, and intimacy. It seems
reasonable to expect that another family member, especially one no
bigger than a bread box, would not disrupt this lifestyle to any great
degree. But, in reality, life after baby does not go on as before.

If you are a parent with visions of perfection, it will be painfully
frustrating to find yourself at twelve noon still in a bathrobe with
beds unmade, laundry up to your elbows, dishes blocking a clear

view of the sink, and a crying baby who seems determined to keep you from doing anything but rocking, feeding, and changing him. Not all days will be this hectic and out of control, but certainly there will be enough of these days to make "perfect parenting" an impossible task.

When both parents work outside the home, the opportunities to fall short of perfection are abundant. The harried mornings, babysitter hassles, overload of housework, frazzled nerves, and short supply of time keep most parents from attaining a state of what they would call normalcy, never mind perfection.

The Reality

No one can be all things to all people. This is especially true of new parents. You cannot, at the same time, consistently be an accomplished parent, housekeeper, and spouse. You can, however, find a comfortable "good enough" balance in all your roles by following these three guidelines:

1. Set Priorities: Because you can't do it all, decide which things you do want to do and which ones you can let go of for now. Is an immaculate house a must for you? Does your garden really need to be manicured? Are gourmet (or even home-cooked) meals a necessity? Take some time to look at the things that fill up your day and knock off the bottom tier of your Must Do list.

2. Lower Your Expectations: How nice it is to know you can stop trying to do it all and still be a good parent. This means you can enjoy your baby and not expect to be full of energy at the end of the day. You don't even have to try to keep your house as neat as you used to. And you can forgive yourself if you get to your in-laws and you find that you're wearing your slippers and your baby's face is covered with dried cereal.

3. Ask for Help: Since you can't do everything that needs to be done each day, it makes sense to ask for help. Tell your spouse how he or she can pitch in; call upon the neighbors and friends who once offered, "Let me know if I can do anything," and let aunts, uncles, and grandparents give you a hand. Asking for help after the birth of your baby doesn't make you a less-than-perfect parent; it makes you a smart one.

MYTH #2
GOOD PARENTS DON'T MAKE MISTAKES

Surely, perfect parents know everything there is to know about child rearing. But real-life parents like you and every other parent you know can't possibly raise children without wondering, at least once a day, "What am I supposed to do now?" All parents, even experienced ones, wonder: Is the baby hungry? Is she cold? How do I stop the hiccups? Why does she spit up so much? It's unrealistic for you to expect to know just what to do every time your baby throws a surprise your way.

The Reality

The quality of your parenting abilities is not judged by how competent you feel. But it is affected by your willingness to admit that you're not always sure of yourself. This is true because hiding your uncertainty leaves you feeling only more uncertain, vulnerable, alone, and teary—certainly not the picture of the good parent you want to be.

Give yourself permission to make mistakes and to admit openly you need help. There's plenty of information available to you, so put aside your illusions of innate perfection and find out what you need to know. Talk to your pediatrician openly and honestly, read child-care books and magazines, talk to other parents who may have found solutions for the problems you're experiencing, and ask advice from the baby's grandparents—they have many years of practical experience they're anxious to share if you ask. Then, finally, rest assured that no one knows everything about raising children. Most parenting skills are learned through daily trial and error.

MYTH #3
PERFECT PARENTS RAISE PERFECT CHILDREN

Some parents believe that their capabilities as a parent are reflected in the actions of their children. Therefore, the logic goes, perfect parents have perfect children. These parents take sole credit for every darling movement their infants display. They take personal pride, for example, in their babies' cute smiles and good medical checkups. On the other hand, they also take complete blame for every action that deviates from wonderful. They claim responsibility, for example, if their babies suffer colic, catch cold, or refuse to smile for Grandma. These feelings often continue throughout the child's early years as parents pat themselves on the back for their children's every good deed and good school grade, and wring their hands in guilt for every backyard fight or teacher's complaint. These parents believe they influence every aspect of their children's lives.

The Reality

Children are unique individuals who do many good and bad things that have nothing to do with their moms' and dads' parenting skills. Some babies cry for no apparent reason and it is not a barometer of parental know-how (see "crying" information in Mistake #4). Other infants are irritable and slow to smile, and it usually has nothing to do with the parents' ability to bond and nurture (see "temperament" information in Mistake #10). And all children grow and mature at different rates, and those who crawl, walk, and talk last are not paragons of parental deprivation. No matter how perfect parents try to mold ideal children, babies will be babies and persistently do things that are not perfect.

Although we can, and should, strive to raise our children to be intelligent, sensitive, moral, creative, personable, caring, and healthy individuals, there is nothing we can do to guarantee that they will exhibit all these characteristics at all times. Infants of even the very best parents will cry out in church, soil their diapers in crowded places, spit up on an admiring aunt's black sweater, and become inconsolable when the photographer says, "Smile." As they grow they will hit their playmates, throw tantrums in supermarkets, knock over potted plants, and vomit in your neighbor's car. When these things happen (and most of them will), you should be ready to assure yourself that they have nothing to do with your abilities as a parent.

These three myths and realities point out clearly the problems of "perfect" parenting. The information probably sounds logical to you, but in practice you may find it difficult to resist the urge to strive for that pinnacle of perfection. If you do try, beware of the consequences: Perfect parenting *is* possible, but only for a short while. After several weeks, or even months, of exhaustive self-sacrificing and relentless giving and caring, you're bound to burn out, explode, or plunge into depression. Perfect parenting is more realistically attained by the parents who find "good enough" ways to take care of their babies and themselves.

Recommended for further reading:

The Superwoman Syndrome
Marjorie Hansen Shaevitz
Warner Books, 1985

Motherhood as Metamorphosis
Joyce Block
Dutton, 1990

Trying to Raise a Superbaby

S itting around the sandbox, clutching thick appointment books, two mothers find it nearly impossible to find a time when their children can get together. "Ben's got play group and French on Monday, gym class on Tuesday, and computer readiness on Thursday," says one mother. "Well, Cole's got drama on Wednesday," says the second. A third, obviously upset mother arrives on the scene and breathlessly explains that her child didn't get into an elite preschool. "If she doesn't get into the right preschool," she says, "she won't get into the right kindergarten. If she doesn't get into the right kindergarten, I can forget about a good prep school and any hope of an Ivy League college. I don't understand it. Her résumé was perfect. Her references were impeccable."

This scene from the 1987 film *Baby Boom* with Diane Keaton parodies the drive some parents feel to create superbabies. Although perhaps an exaggeration, it certainly gives a clear picture of this highly competitive aspect of parenting. Why, we might wonder, do parents push their children into swimming, skiing, and piano lessons before they are even old enough to walk? And, we wonder, should we be doing the same?

The first question of why parents push their children to excel in areas beyond their years is not easily answered because we raise our children in ways that are the result of many factors. However, social researchers have uncovered three possible causes for this age of the superbaby:

Ego

No matter how vigorously we deny it, we often see our children as a reflection of ourselves. "If my child is perceived as smart, so will I be," the theory goes. We also tend to see our children as a barometer of the success or failure of our ability to parent: "If my child obediently follows directions and excels in gymnastics," we might feel, "the other parents will think I'm a good parent." And last, our ego can make us feel totally responsible for our child's every success and failure. This makes us especially vulnerable to entrepreneurs eager to exploit our parental emotions.

Competition

In our fast-paced society, we value competence and independence. Many of us have learned that we reach these goals only through hard work and a relentless game of one-upmanship. We compete to get good jobs, to get promotions, to be the best parents, and sometimes, to have the best children. If other one-month-olds are learning to appreciate classical music, so will ours. If other toddlers are enhancing their coordination skills in gymnastic class, so must ours. And if other children are learning French at the age of eighteen months, so can ours. Staying one up on the Joneses keeps many parents and babies very busy.

Confusion

If it's true, as some family, friends, and educators tell us, that only the first and the best achieve success in the race of life, do we dare risk not pushing our little ones toward the finish line? What if Ivy League schools do take only graduates of the most prestigious nursery schools—can we afford to give in to our gut feelings that say the long-term influence of any nursery school diploma is nil? Professional programs such as the Better Baby Institute, and books like *How to Give Your Baby Encyclopedic Knowledge,* and places like Better Baby Stores that sell computers and musical instruments (but no toys) surely make us wonder if we are neglecting our parental responsibility if we do not cram full the minds of our babies. And so we go along with the superbaby trend, perhaps feeling, all the time, that something isn't quite right.

EXPERT ADVICE

For whatever reasons, many parents are ignoring the growing bulk of professional opinion that is solidly against efforts to foster superbabies. The American Pediatric Association, for example, has advised parents against infant swimming lessons, yet there are waiting lists for these lessons all over the country. Five major organizations including the International Reading Association and the National Association for the Education of Young Children have pointed out the risks of teaching academic subjects to young children; yet still, books like *How to Teach Your Baby to Read* continually make the best-seller lists. This decision to ignore professional advice is a mistake that far too many new parents make.

It's true that infants are more than helpless lumps of protoplasm. They can learn academic subjects at a most tender age (some say math can be learned at seven months and reading at eleven months), but the question you need to ask yourself is: To what advantage? Does a one-year-old have any real interest in learning that the furry animal who licks his face and is soft to hug is spelled D-O-G?

Besides offering no practical purpose from the child's viewpoint, there is no evidence that intense early learning provides any lasting educational advantages. Instead, accelerated learning situations often turn education into a dreadful chore, completed only to obtain adult approval. Yes, the very young can learn to spell words and add numbers, but concentration on these kinds of specific skills teaches them, more notably, to mimic rather than to learn through self-motivation, interest, and curiosity.

Dr. David Elkind, author of *The Hurried Child,* believes emphatically that education is not a race. He feels that studying the wrong things at too early an age constitutes miseducation, putting children at risk for short-term stress and long-term learning problems—for no purpose.[1] Many child psychologists support this belief especially now that long-term studies are finding that early learners who were pushed to succeed often become nervous and stressed, and have low self-esteem and poor social skills.

Although it is astounding to listen to a three-year-old competently play the violin, recite Shakespeare, or reconstruct elaborate mathematical models, these performances can also be viewed as evidence of misdirected energies. Paying too much attention to specific skills at such early ages interferes with the more essential lessons of the first few years. In the first year alone, babies carry an exceptionally heavy course load. They learn to build attachments to others, to differentiate familiar from foreign, and to decipher the concept of object permanence. They also learn how to use their bodies to sit, stand, crawl, and walk. Their minds begin to grasp the elements of problem solving and the intricacies of understanding, interpreting, and speaking our language. Above all, they are very busy learning how to learn.

RAISING "SMART" BABIES

Without creating a superbaby, you can nurture and love your child in ways that have been proven to promote intellectual growth. The following guidelines will show you that it's easy to introduce your baby to the fun of learning.

Stimulate

Babies need stimulation to learn how to interact with their world in constructive ways. Although they may seem content to lie around staring into space, they depend on you to supply some daily excitement. Excitement for an infant can be as simple as being "where the action is." When you move from room to room, for example, bring your baby with you; let him watch your day-to-day routine. It may seem mundane to you, but to your baby it's fascinating.

You can also stimulate your baby by encouraging visual investigation and exploration. Contrary to popular belief, infants can see their world, in color, from the minute they are born. At birth this vision is a bit blurry, but by two to three weeks it becomes quite clear. At this stage, infants prefer primary to pastel colors, and high-contrast black-and-white patterns to objects, like stuffed animals, with hazy borders. Although infants can see objects near and far, their attention span is so short that they tend to notice only things within a few feet of their face. At two to five months, babies gain mature depth perception and enjoy more distant visual stimulation. They may intently watch a mobile, smile at a familar face across the room, and can track moving objects. When you decorate your baby's environment, keep this information in mind. Although soft and pretty pastels may appeal to you, your baby will be more motivated to look at and examine items that are blue, red, green, or black and white. In these colors, mobiles, crib bumpers, and toys can be more than just cute nursery decorations.

As your baby grows, you can continue to stimulate curiosity by allowing space for exploration. Of course, you'll lock many doors and cabinets to keep fragile and dangerous objects out of reach, but leave some baby-proofed drawers and closets and even rooms open for investigation.

As they grow, toddlers don't need structured lessons for intellectual stimulation. Give them a kitchen table full of paper, paints, markers, crayons, yarn, glue, or clay and they'll have more than enough stimulation for the day.

Assist

Babies don't need you to do *everything* for them; very often they need only a little help. When your babies reach for objects, for example, you can promote a sense of accomplishment by not giving it to them, but rather letting them grab it themselves. Or, when they try to hold their own bottles, encourage the effort. Then as your children grow, try to refrain from jumping in and taking over. Even though you can do a job or project better and quicker, if your children are not complaining, let them work it out alone. If they want to dress themselves, let them. A shirt worn backward for a few hours is no big deal; the sense of pride and achievement that it gives young children is a big deal. And when you plan an outing to the park, for example, don't plan every minute. Leave plenty of time to allow your children to pursue their own agenda and use their interests to guide your activities.

Expose

It's easy to assume that there's no point in taking babies anywhere special because they'll never remember it anyway. Although it's true that in our conscious memory, events before the age of five are few, in our unconscious, everything that has ever happened makes up who we are and how we perceive the world.

Feeling the texture of sand at the beach, sitting on Dad's lap for a scary yet exhilarating sleigh ride, hiking while perched high in a back carrier, enjoying the colors and sounds of a parade, all of these things, and the adventures of every day as well, may not be recalled at a later time, but don't underestimate their influence on your children's development. Never turn down an opportunity to expose your children to new things solely because you think "they won't understand what's going on anyway." They need to see and hear and touch and taste all that they can because nurturing curiosity will foster an eagerness to learn. All these experiences will build one upon the other and then the child will grow believing not that flashcards can teach multiplication but that life is full of fascinating and enjoyable things.

Talk

Talking is so fundamentally vital in raising a "smart" child that we have given the subject its own chapter. See Mistake #11 to learn why communication between parent and infant is a cornerstone of child development.

The last word in raising a true superbaby is *enjoyment.* Better to spend infancy bouncing, babbling, and laughing than to focus solely on IQ enhancement.

Recommended for further reading:

The Too Precious Child
Lynne Williams, Henry Berman, and Louisa Rose
Warner Books, 1987

The Hurried Child
David Elkind
Addison-Wesley, 1989

Underestimating the Value of Infant Play

Two-month-old Brooke sat in her infant seat contentedly watching her older brother play with his blocks. "Look at Brooke's face," whispered Yvette to her husband. "She really looks like she'd love to get right in there and play with Ryan." "Yeah," smiled Ned. "I can't wait till she's older. I'll bet she's gonna be a lot of fun."

Yvette and Ned's assumption that their infant is too young to play is a common underestimation of an infant's needs and capabilities. Play is the work of childhood. Children don't play just to pass the time; it is through play that they learn about their world, about what things can and cannot do, and about how their bodies work. Through games, playthings, toys, books, and songs parents can challenge their babies to explore life and to master elementary skills. This exploration can and should begin shortly after birth in ways that stimulate the senses and develop motor skills. You may find, as an added bonus, that because play can satisfy an infant's need for stimulation and reduces boredom, your infant will cry less each day.

The following play activities will give you an idea of the kinds of things infants like to do. You'll find four hundred more activities that stimulate creativity, encourage self-confidence, and improve coordination in the book recommended at the end of this chapter.

BIRTH TO NINE WEEKS

For the first two months, most infants lay with their heads turned toward the side. Take advantage of that fact and place an unbreakable mirror in your baby's crib or playpen at eye level about eight to twelve inches from his face. Most infants are fascinated by the human face; what better face to admire than his own.

Music is an all-time infant favorite. Experiment with all kinds of music, from Beethoven to Raffi, and watch how your baby responds to each. If you find one type that seems particularly appealing, use a cassette recording to offer the fun of sound over and over again. Your baby might also enjoy a waltz around the room or the sound of your own crooning.

Infants are most attracted to vivid primary colors or black-and-white contrast designs. When you buy toys, keep this in mind. Even if your baby isn't yet ready to "play" with the toy, she will enjoy visually examining it and following its movements and sounds.

Make time each day for unrestrained kicking and wiggling. There are, of course, times when babies must be tied into infant seats, strollers, carseats, and highchairs, but during playtime let your infant lie on a blanketed floor to stretch and wiggle and kick as you offer your smiling face and exclamations as reward.

Babies are never too young to profit from a good story. Read to your baby. You'll find that even an infant will sometimes become enraptured with the rhythm of nursery rhymes.

TWO TO FOUR MONTHS

Two-month-olds are ready to enjoy a mobile hung over the crib. These infants are now able to hold their heads steady and straight and enjoy the movement and sound of this toy.

Between two and four months of age, your baby will be ready to become physically involved in playtime. As your baby begins to grasp and swing at objects, he will become fascinated by toys that are suspended just within reach of outstretched arms. Crib gyms and toy bars are most fun at this age.

When babies discover they have feet, a whole vista of play possibilities opens up. They can now kick at suspended toys or inflated beach balls. You can encourage your baby to grab for her toes by using brightly colored socks, ribbons, or bells on the feet.

Once babies learn to grasp, hold, and manipulate objects they can advance in their play activities. Rather than solely visually enjoying their toys, they can shake, drop, bang, and bite them. Teething rings and rattles are especially fun playthings.

FOUR TO SIX MONTHS

At this age you'll get delightful feedback from your baby. This is a time of giggles and hearty laughs. In addition to the mirror, rattles, and crib gyms, tickling games become most exciting. Tummy kisses are an all-time favorite, as are walking fingers that gently climb from the tummy to chin and end with a tickle.

SIX TO TWELVE MONTHS

These babies are anxious to find their fun while in motion. They creep and crawl to grasp, kick, and swipe at their favorite toys. They also love bath toys, especially ones that fill with water and pour out again. Peek-a-boo and hide-and-seek around a large chair are knee-slapping fun that help teach object permanence. And of course, all doors, drawers, and cabinets are now fair game for play (and a good reason to baby-proof all rooms !). As your baby approaches toddler-hood, you'll find it easy to play games and to incorporate play into your daily schedule.

WARNING

Playing with infants encourages healthy physical and mental development, but there are a few words of caution that need to be mentioned. Do not play with your babies by bouncing them excessively or throwing them into the air. A baby's neck is relatively weak and prone to injuries such as whiplash. Tossing can also cause retina detachment, which can lead to serious eye problems. Jostling or shaking a baby is also dangerous. Emergency room physicians have reported increasing numbers of infants suffering from what they now call "Shaken Baby Syndrome." These babies who have been shaken excessively (both in anger and in play) can suffer brain damage and internal bleeding, as well as spinal cord and eye damage.

You are your infant's first playmate. Seize this opportunity to enjoy your child, teach the thrill of exploration, and encourage the development of cognitive and motor skills.

Recommended for further reading:

Your Child at Play: Birth to One Year
Marilyn Segal
Newmarket Press, 1986

Ignoring Yourself

C arla's day was as hectic as always. It started at dawn when six-month-old David screamed out the morning alarm. After the mad rush to wake, wash, eat, and dress, Carla drove her three-year-old to preschool, and then came home to make the beds, feed and change the baby, throw in the laundry, and strain a bowl of peas for David's lunch. Later that night, when the third load of laundry was folded and the last supper dishes were washed, Carla realized that she had not eaten anything all day or returned the promised phone call to a good friend. Well, no time now, she thought, Jenny needs a bath, David needs to be changed, and I promised I'd read them the end of their bedtime story before I return the book to the library tomorrow. Finally, at 9 P.M., Carla flopped on the couch and listened for a moment to the silence of sleeping children. But no time to slack off, she remembered. Her husband would be hungry when he got home, the toys in the living room needed to be cleaned up, and she still wanted to measure and cut David's curtains.

Obviously, Carla is working hard at being a good mother and housewife. However, as admirable as her efforts may appear, she is foolishly ignoring her own needs. This sacrifice of self may eventually make it impossible for her to fully enjoy her children and husband.

In the after-childbirth struggle to do what's best for everybody else, many parents ignore their own needs and give up everything that isn't "baby" related. Some parents (especially new moms) put aside all their hobbies, activities, friends, and interests; they focus so intently on the all-important child that they forget to nurture themselves. They may even jump into the stereotyped role of the "perfect" parent who bakes breads and cookies, sews and knits, and cleans and nurtures in every spare second. For some parents, this is a satisfying change of lifestyle. But most parents eventually find that being a full-time martyr is an unsatisfying and tiring business.

Ignoring your own needs can cause you to neglect parts of your life that are vital to a healthy existence. You may overlook physical needs like eating nutritious foods because you're too busy making formula, expressing milk, or bathing the baby, and because there's laundry to do or beds to be made you feel you certainly can't rest when your baby naps. You may disregard emotional needs because you can't bear time away from the baby to arrange a "date" with your spouse, or you feel you can't socialize if it means taking your attention away from your baby and parenting duties. You may also slight psychological needs by dumping old interests and friends and putting a halt to all activities that don't focus on the baby. When physical, emotional, and psychological needs are repeatedly ignored, new parents become prime candidates for the New Parent Stress Syndrome (explained in Mistake #1), which interferes with the enjoyable aspects of parenthood.

The truth is, parenthood is not all-fulfilling. It doesn't make physiological or psychological sense to even try to make it so. Every parent needs rest, recreation, and self-nurturing in order to have the energy and spirit to give willingly to others. Studies repeatedly find that happy and self-fulfilled parents are the ones who are most capable of enjoying and loving their children. No one can constantly give, give, give, and still maintain a sense of love and joy without taking something back. Use the following guidelines to help you balance the time you give to your baby and the attention you give to yourself.

1. Take time every day for *you*. The busier you feel, the more necessary it is to have this "alone" time. When the baby naps, stay away from housework; do something for you—rest, read a book, have a cup of tea, or anything else that you would enjoy. When you can get out without the baby, do it; call a friend (this includes your spouse), take a walk, join an exercise club. Keep in touch with your before-baby interests because keeping your own life vital and stimulating will give you more personal joy to give back to your family.

2. Eat a nutritious diet. Skimping on your need for fuel and energy will not improve your ability to be a good parent. Also, the postpartum period of physical and psychological readjustment is not a good time to go on a crash diet to lose your pregnancy weight. Poor nutrition fosters feelings of fatigue and encourages the onset of depression.

If you feel you have time to eat only whatever you can hold in one hand and eat on the run, you'll be glad to hear that hurried and stressed people can better keep up their energy if they eat small portions every two to three hours throughout the day. This reduces fatigue and tension by maintaining an optimum blood sugar level. To reduce feelings of anxiety, you should also restrict your intake of caffeine by cutting back on soda, coffee, tea, and chocolate.

3. Exercise regularly. The suggestion that exercise is an antidote to many postbaby problems usually receives a reception of groans and stares of disbelief from tired and overwhelmed parents. But because exercise can actually restore depleted energy reserves, it can give you back a sense of physical well-being. Exercise also serves to get you out of the baby-care rut; it takes your mind off the baby for a while and, if you can leave the baby behind, it gets you out of the house and involved with other adults.

4. Meet with other parents. New parents often feel they always have to appear as if parenthood is just the best thing that ever happened to them. But when they have a chance to meet with other parents, the truth about insecurities, worries, and frustrations comes pouring out. Talking to people who have experienced the same feelings and circumstances as you is an often-used form of support therapy. Camaraderie has a way of putting things into perspective and removing the feeling of "everybody else can do this with ease, except me."

If you can't easily arrange casual conversations with other parents in your neighborhood or family, look for an organized group to join. Call the local hospital or YWCA or ask your pediatrician if such a support group is available to you. Search until you find a group, or perhaps you can put together one of your own. Sharing the disappointments, as well as the joys, of child rearing is an effective way to pamper your psychological need for support and adult interaction.

5. Consider your own needs when you make decisions. When you're weighing the pros and cons of returning to work, or taking on an extra project, or hiring a babysitter, consider not only what's best for your baby but also how you feel and what would be best for you. For the first few months, your infant child will be perfectly content as long as you feed, bathe, change, and nurture her. All the other decisions you make should reduce, not add to, your daily burdens of guilt, fatigue, and obligation.

6. Accept yourself for who you are. Like most of us, you probably are not the perfect parent. You probably cannot give unconditional love day after day without getting tired and angry. You may even experience times when you regret having this child. These feelings occur to all parents at one time or another. But always remember that you are someone who counts in the family equation of health and happiness. If you let yourself fall into the ignored-parent trap and become overtired, overworked, and overwhelmed, you won't ever know the full spectrum of joy that parenting can give. Take care of yourself so you can give your baby the gift of a healthy, happy parent who looks forward to each day of parenting.

Recommended for further reading:

A Good Enough Parent
Bruno Bettelheim
Vintage Books, 1988

Struggling Alone with the Blues

I t was 6:15 in the morning when Darlene heard one-month-old Kirstie cry out from the nursery. She pulled the covers up over her head and prayed that the crying would stop. I can't do this again, she thought. Please, someone else take care of this child. I can't do it again today. For the past month Darlene has felt increasingly tired and unhappy. She sometimes finds herself staring at her baby—the child she had longed for—and wondering how she could feel so detached from her own flesh and blood. This day would be especially trying because her husband was once again off on a business trip. "Why did I let him talk me into moving so far from home when he's never here anyway," Darlene mumbled to herself as she left her bed and headed toward the drudgery of another day.

Darlene doesn't know it, but she's suffering from a common consequence of childbirth called postpartum depression (PPD). Like so many other new mothers, Darlene is suffering alone because she doesn't recognize the seriousness of the problem and doesn't know there is a remedy. Unfortunately, while she struggles alone with the pain of depression, fatigue, and confusion, her self-esteem will plummet, her attitude toward parenting will sour, and her relationship with her child will become strained and may even become abusive. New mothers who recognize the symptoms of PPD are much more likely to get help and save themselves and their babies from the trials of untreated depression.

WHAT IS POSTPARTUM DEPRESSION?

Postpartum depression is a blanket term commonly used to describe a wide range of unhappy feelings experienced by women after the birth of a baby. A more specific definition of PPD and identification of its exact causes are currently the subjects of numerous medical and psychological studies. Until more is known, however, PPD is generally broken into three different categories. Although their causes and symptoms sometimes overlap, new mothers should know the general characteristics of each so they do not make the mistake of ignoring "blue" feelings and trying to deal with them alone.

The three categories of PPD are explained in this chapter. At the end of the chapter are a number of preventative measures you should be aware of to ensure that a little case of the blues doesn't escalate into something that will disrupt your relationship with your baby and jeopardize your own physical and mental health.

BABY BLUES

The mildest form of PPD affects 50 to 80 percent of all new mothers and is often called "Baby Blues." The blues generally begin three to seven days after childbirth and disappear without medical intervention in five to twenty-one days.

Symptoms

The Baby Blues symptoms can include:

fatigue	anxiety
frequent crying	confusion
mood swings	feelings of insecurity
nervousness	detachment from baby

At this mild level of PPD, new mothers generally cannot pinpoint why they are experiencing these symptoms. When asked what's wrong, they'll usually answer, "Nothing." When asked why they're crying, they'll reply, "I don't know."

Causes

Most medical experts agree that Baby Blues are caused by dramatic physiological changes that occur in hormonal levels after birth. (Levels of estrogen and progesterone drop as much as tenfold!) Social factors such as lack of family support and psychological factors such as marital tension can also play a role in causing and/or aggravating this mild form of PPD.

Treatment

Baby Blues generally go away without any form of treatment, but because mild depression can escalate into more severe forms, even a simple case of the blues should not be completely ignored. Most often, the suggestions in Mistake #17 that help new mothers focus attention on themselves are just what's needed to outsmart the blues. Most important are factors that give you plenty of emotional support, rest, exercise, and good nutrition.

MODERATE POSTPARTUM DEPRESSION

The after-baby condition frequently labeled postpartum depression is a moderate-range depression that affects one in ten new mothers. It can develop at almost any time up to one year after childbirth, but most often it appears sometime between the second week and third month after birth. Typically, it can last anywhere from several weeks to several months.

Symptoms

Moderate PPD symptoms can include:

constant depression	fatigue
low self-esteem	disturbed sleep
loss of appetite	lost sexual interest
confusion	difficulty making decisions
feeling overwhelmed	difficulty concentrating

These symptoms differ from those of the Baby Blues in that the depressing feelings are constant and women can generally pinpoint specific reasons they feel unhappy, inept, or discouraged. A woman may, for example, point to the crying of a colicky baby, the temperament of a difficult infant, or the drastic lifestyle change from career woman to homemaker.

Causes

Moderate PPD is apparently rooted in negative social and psychological factors. These tensions may include the daily stresses of parenting, feelings of isolation, a colicky infant, chronic lack of sleep, and marital tensions. Women who experience moderate PPD have a one in five chance of recurrence after future pregnancies.

Treatment

Moderate PPD is best treated with professional help. It often responds well to a combination of antidepressant drugs and cognitive therapy that teaches women to better cope with the stress of parenthood. The speed and degree of recovery depends, of course, on successful identification of the cause and the willingness of the woman to take action to remedy it.

Emotional support from spouse, family, and friends is also a vital component in the treatment of this midrange depression.

If left untreated, moderate PPD may lead to a loss of enthusiasm and energy and strained parent/child relations. If a month or two go by and you are not yet feeling any enthusiasm about motherhood, or if you still aren't experiencing normal eating and sleeping patterns, you should call your doctor or the support group given at the end of this chapter. In rare cases, the symptoms persist and greatly increase in severity; this may indicate the onset of the most serious form of postpartum depression, called postpartum psychosis.

POSTPARTUM PSYCHOSIS

Postpartum psychosis is a severe state of depression that affects only one in every one thousand new mothers. Its symptoms generally appear three to thirty days after birth and if left untreated may continue for years.

Symptoms

In addition to the symptoms experienced by women suffering moderate PPD, postpartum psychosis symptoms include:

hallucinations
frightening feelings and thoughts
overconcern for the baby
thoughts of suicide
thoughts of doing harm to the baby
delusions
hearing voices that suggest the baby is evil
occasionally, violent behavior

Causes

This most severe form of depression seems to be linked to physiological and biochemical changes in the body. Most affected women have a personal or family history of mental illness.

Treatment

Postpartum psychosis absolutely requires professional intervention. Some women respond well to counseling and/or antipsychotic medication such as Thorazine®. Others need hospitalization and more intensive treatment and monitoring.

PREVENTIVE STRATEGIES

Knowing the risk factors, general symptoms, and prevention tactics associated with postpartum depression will help you avoid the seemingly endless pain of suffering alone at a time in your life that should be filled with joy and pleasure.

Risk Factors

Although it is impossible to predict with complete accuracy which pregnant women will become depressed after childbirth, experts have noted a number of factors that indicate a higher-than-average risk. These include:

- a personal history of mood swings
- an unwanted pregnancy
- a difficult pregnancy that included bouts of morning sickness and backaches
- an exceptionally easy pregnancy that builds up expectations of "easy" parenting
- a long, difficult, unsupported, or complicated labor
- a birth experience that failed to fulfill expectations
- delivering a premature or health-compromised baby
- expectations of perfection in parenting

General Symptoms

If you experience any of the following feelings after the birth or adoption of a child, you may be suffering postpartum depression:

- crying for no apparent reason
- feelings of inadequacy
- no feelings for the baby
- changes in sleep patterns
- anxiety
- helplessness
- anger
- inability to cope
- depression that may range from a lack of concentration to sadness to thoughts of suicide

If you experience several of these symptoms, be sure to follow the preventive tactics explained below. If these symptoms persist or increase in severity, be sure to seek professional help.

Prevention Tactics

If you are aware of having several risk factors and are experiencing some of the general symptoms listed above, you can best confront the problem by following these two steps:

1. Take care of yourself. Learn to recognize your overload factors and avoid them. If you feel you can't keep the house clean *and* take care of the baby, let the house go (see Mistake #14 for suggestions that will help you avoid the superparent trap). If your baby has colic or a difficult temperament read and follow the advice in this book that explains how to better deal with these stresses (see Mistakes #3 and #10). As you adjust to the stress of new parenthood, practice the stress-reduction techniques described in Mistake #1. And, most especially, take time for self-nurturing (see Mistake #17). In fact, every chapter in this book has been written with the goal of helping you find bliss in raising your baby and avoid the pitfalls that cause unhappiness. Use the advice that best fits into your daily routine to take care of *you*, first and foremost and above all else. When you do this, you'll have the emotional and physical strength you need to take care of all your other responsibilities.

2. Seek support. Do not try to handle your negative feelings alone. These feelings do not mean that you are a bad mother; they do not in any way indicate that you can't handle motherhood. They are *very* common feelings shared, to some degree, by approximately eight out of ten new mothers—the majority of whom turn out to be wonderful parents.

Talk to your spouse. He can't understand your feelings and actions unless you explain what's going on. His emotional support is very important to your ability to overcome your problem. Ask him for that help.

Talk to other mothers. Sharing your frustrations lessens their load, and hearing about similar experiences will take away some of the horror and mystery of this trying period.

Seek counseling in group therapy or organized support groups. Trained counselors and women who have experienced postpartum depression can, through sharing, caring, and working together, help you find healthy ways of coping with your feelings. One organization that strives to support women who are suffering from postpartum depression is called Depression After Delivery (DAD). This Pennsylvania-based group is a network of close to ten thousand women around the country who field phone calls and dispense information and educational materials, provide referrals, and just plain listen. If you're feeling down, give them a call at (215) 295-3994.

Recommended for further reading:

The New Mother Syndrome
Carol Dix
Doubleday, 1985

Slighting Grandparents

Meg and Don prepared to leave two-month-old Alicia and five-year-old Ashley overnight with Meg's parents so they could attend a friend's out-of-town wedding. In careful detail, Meg wrote down each child's schedule; she noted how much formula Alicia should drink at what times of day and even her best burping position. She gave explicit diapering directions and noted naptimes and soothing techniques that would help lull the baby off to sleep. Ashley's set of directions included a list of forbidden foods and TV shows. It gave her a bedtime of 8:30 P.M. and presented a suggested bedtime reading list.

The next day, after the children said their good-byes to Grandma and Grandpa, Meg asked Ashley how she enjoyed her stay with her grandparents. "It was great!" Ashley cheered. "As soon as you left, Grandma threw away that piece of paper you gave her and we had a TV party with candy and soda. Grandma even let Alicia eat some of her chocolate bar. And we all stayed up real late until Alicia and I fell asleep on the couch. When can I stay there again?"

Meg and Don were furious. How dare Meg's parents blatantly ignore their wishes! Meg immediately called her mother. They argued for twenty minutes and then abruptly hung up in anger. The two did not speak to each other for the next ten days. Ashley and Alicia, of course, did not see their grandparents during this time and may never again enjoy a sleepover.

Like Meg and Don, all new parents struggle for independence from their own parents and may find the separation fraught with arguments and hurt feelings. But if you are fortunate enough to have accessible parents who want to be involved with their grandchildren, it will be well worth your while to find a way to work out your differences and use grandparents as a one-of-a-kind resource on which you can always rely.

In addition to offering free babysitting service, grandparents can provide your children with things more priceless. They give children an extended family identity that passes on family history, beliefs, and values. They can serve as a role model of involved and caring grandparents, and they also give children an opportunity to learn respect for the elderly. Above all, they can offer the greatest benefit of unconditional love. Without much responsibility, disciplinary ties, or ego involvement, grandparents can be loving and indulgent in ways that most parents cannot be but from which children greatly benefit. With so much to gain, fostering a strong bond between child and grandparent should be a priority in all homes.

Like parenting, grandparenting doesn't always come easy. There are many ways in which parents and grandparents come into conflict. Child rearing styles may clash. Grandma may have more experience with treating a stuffy nose, but Mom may be more up to date on the better remedy. Grandpa may feel it's his right to spoil his grandchild, but Dad may resent the flagrant disregard of family rules. Grandparents may vocalize against mothers working outside the home, making Mom feel angry and guilty. Or Grandma may be an active or employed woman herself, who doesn't want to be an on-call babysitter. Sometimes one set of grandparents feels slighted when the other grandparents have more opportunities to see the grandchildren. Quite clearly, the occasions for anger, hurt feelings, and resentment are numerous in the parent/grandparent arena. But for the sake of your children it is important to work to make the grandparent/child relationship flourish.

You can more easily do this by following these basic guidelines:

1. Ensure that, when possible, all involved grandparents have opportunities to bond with your infant. Just as parent/child bonding takes time and some effort, so will grandparent/child bonding. Don't just hand off your baby to grandparents like a hot potato and grab it back. Give them time to hold and touch the child. Let the baby get accustomed to the sound of their voices and feel of their arms. Leave grandparent and infant alone for a while; just as you and your baby need time together, so do the baby and his grandparents.

2. If the grandparents live far away and don't see their grandchildren often, help them know the child by communicating regularly through letters, pictures, and even videos. Encourage them to send a cassette tape on which they talk, read rhymes, or sing to the baby. Then play it for your child, so she can become acquainted with their voices. When the grandparents do visit, the baby will feel they are familiar.

3. Let grandparents offer you advice and guidance. Some aspects of raising and loving children are never outdated and so their experience may be helpful to you. You may later choose not to follow any of their suggestions, but at least give them the courtesy of listening.

4. Keep disagreements off a personal level. Calmly explain that your methods and choices follow doctor's orders or "expert-approved" techniques you've read in child-care books or articles. Then share your reading resources with the grandparents. This will help them learn what's new and recommended and may help them better understand your style of parenting.

5. Don't disagree with an in-law grandparent and expect your spouse to take sides on the spot. Privately discuss your approach and beliefs with your spouse and present a united front to the grandparents. Fighting "your" family and "my" family battles serves no purpose that can benefit your child.

6. Consider the circumstances before you make hard and fast rules. If the grandparents visit only occasionally, for example, without comment, you may be able to let them be overindulgent. But if they visit quite often, you may need to sit down and talk about your family rules and reach a mutual understanding about how things like discipline or food selection will be mutually handled.

7. Consider that continuous clashes with your parents may have more to do with unresolved issues from your own childhood. Establish your place as an adult in the family by responding as an adult, not as an angry child.

8. When the grandparents choose to ignore your wishes and spoil their grandchildren, don't fly off the handle. Most often your child won't suffer any damage when grandparents throw away all the rules and follow their hearts rather than your instructions.

Grandparents are made to be advocates for kids. It's their role and privilege to spoil and love indulgently. With tolerance and perseverance, you can allow your children an emotional attachment that will add a unique fullness to their lives, a bequest certainly worth the effort.

Recommended for further reading:

Grandparenting
David Elkind
Scott, Foresman and Company, 1989

Grandparents, Grandchildren: The Vital Connection
Arthur Kornhaber and Kenneth Woodward
Transaction Publishers, 1984

Grandparents can find support and advice through either of these two organizations:
Foundation for Grandparenting
This organization offers a free copy of its newletter, "Vital Connections." Send a legal-size self-addressed stamped envelope to PO Box 31, Lake Placid, NY 12946.

Grandparents as Parents (GAP)
This organization will help you network with other grandparents in your area. Write Sylvie de Toledo, Psychiatric Clinic for Youth, 2801 Atlantic Avenue, Long Beach, CA 90801, (213) 595-3151.

Misunderstanding Siblings

Three-year-old Johnny was thrilled to have a new little sister. "When Christa came home from the hospital six months ago," their mom remembers, "Johnny was gentle and kind and he really enjoyed having a baby to look after. But now . . . I don't dare leave them alone for a minute. He hits her and throws toys at her whenever he thinks I'm not looking."

Yesterday, Johnny's mom found him inside his sister's crib ready to pitch her over the side. "I guess Johnny is jealous of the attention the baby gets," she told her friend, "but one of these days he's really going to hurt her. So *again* I yelled at him and sent him to his room. How can I make him be nice to his sister?"

The appearance of a new baby can cause feelings of great insecurity and loss in siblings. Like Johnny, your older child may react at first with loving enthusiasm or perhaps even indifference to the new arrival, but once the reality of coexistence sets in, he may act up in negative ways that are guaranteed to get your full attention. You can better understand the intensity of the negative feelings a first-born feels through this often-used analogy: Imagine your reaction should your spouse bring home a new marriage partner and announce that all three of you are going to live together and it's going to be fun. After assuring you that you both will be loved equally and you both are important members of the family, your spouse asks you to love the new family member, share your things, and accept that you won't get as much attention as you used to because you can take care of yourself now. How would you feel? Keep this feeling in mind if you observe the common reactions of siblings detailed below.

NEGATIVE BEHAVIORS TOWARD PARENTS

Many studies have examined the reactions of young children to the birth of a brother or sister. All have found a significant number who become exceptionally disobedient and demanding (especially toward the mother). Many children are quick to realize that playing quietly by themselves won't attract their parents' attention and so they cleverly devise loud, obnoxious, and often destructive ways to guarantee themselves quick (albeit negative) attention.

In addition, children often display a notable increase in tearfulness, clinging, and whining. Although obvious signs of insecurity, these actions can be very annoying to new parents who don't have the time, patience, or energy to deal with this kind of "babyish" behavior.

Some children try to "punish" their parents (or themselves) by acting withdrawn and sullen. "If nobody wants to love me anymore," they reason, "I'll just pretend they don't exist and go off quietly to live by myself; then they'll be sorry."

We all have our unique ways of responding to hurtful situations. Don't be surprised if your child chooses to react by acting out against you through disobedient, demanding, clinging, or withdrawal behaviors. A first-born who hits his mom and screams "I hate you" is doing the only thing he can think of at that moment to express his pain and ask for assurances of love.

NEGATIVE BEHAVIORS TOWARD THE BABY

You know it would be difficult for you to "be nice" to your spouse's new marriage partner, so keep this in mind when you ask the same of your older child. Some children try to hurt the new baby by hitting, slapping, pinching, et cetera, but most know this would displease you and so use more indirect methods of inflicting pain or discomfort. These children use subtle "getting even" tactics that can include deliberately shaking or startling a sleeping baby with excuses like "I wanted to say hi." Others will take away the blanket or bottle, and many will overwhelm the baby with painful bear hugs, high-pressured kisses, or crushing head rubs.

Whether intentional or not, it is not uncommon for young children to physically harm newborns. So, obviously, they should not be left alone together or left unsupervised. Loving and well-meaning siblings can harm infants by picking them up incorrectly, or by dropping or smothering them. Curious children can easily harm babies because they consider things such as "If I push the end of this spoon into one ear, will it come out the other ear?" And, of course, jealous children can (with what they believe is good reason) try to get rid of the intruder by hiding her in the closet. These behaviors are not at all uncommon, so don't expect your children to "be nice" when you're not looking.

REGRESSION

Your first-born will quickly realize that babies get priority attention because they are virtually helpless and must have everything done for them. So, simple logic tells your child that he can better hold on to your love by being a baby. That's why it's common for older children to regress to infantile behaviors: they may use baby talk or a baby bottle, crawl or suck their thumb, cry to be carried, or even relapse in their toileting skills. If, when this happens, you can avoid scolding your child or making him feel guilty (as explained below) you'll find that this period of regression will subside on its own.

DO AND DON'T GUIDELINES

There is nothing you can do that will make your children welcome their new brother or sister with heartfelt warmth and love. But you can ease their insecurities and, at the same time, make your own adjustment in dual-parenting less stressful by following these Do and Don't Guidelines:

Do

Do help your child balance the disadvantages of having a new baby in the house with a few special advantages. Make sure you lavish your child with affection and reassurances. This is also a good time to give out privileges such as staying up a bit later at night, hearing an extra story at bedtime, or getting another cookie at snack time. Don't worry about spoiling or overdoing it; remember that at this point in time you can barely hope to give all your children *equal* time.

Do find time to be alone with your older child. As you schedule doctor visits, baths, and feedings for the baby, schedule special time with your first-born too. Even fifteen minutes of daily undivided attention will help balance the scales of sibling justice. Also, a once-a-week solo excursion to the park, a restaurant, or the zoo will give her something to look forward to and will make the time you spend with the new baby seem a bit more bearable.

Do encourage your older child to help you care for the baby. Children feel especially excluded and ignored during bath and feeding times when you must focus your attention so intently on the baby. So welcome your child's assistance, and teach him how to be Mommy and Daddy's helper (even though sometimes it may really make extra work for you!).

Don't

Don't push your child's development to accommodate the new baby. Encouraging your first-born to be a "big" boy or girl can work against your goal to offer reassurance because growing up can be a frightening idea, especially to preschool children. Bigness can mean independence, responsibility, and learning to fend for themselves— all those things that they worry will keep your attention focused on the baby instead of them. Unless you've already successfully started, this is not the time for weaning, toilet training, or changing from a crib to a bed. These changes will often worsen an already frightful time.

Don't scold your child for verbally expressing her displeasure at the baby's arrival. If you insist that your older child accept and love the baby, you may establish an implied restriction on voicing true feelings. Then you'll find, as in all life situations, that pent-up emotions eventually do find their way out—but often with destructive results. You give your children permission to voice negative feelings when you don't act shocked if they admit to hating the baby or wanting to send it back. You can even lead them in honest discussions by acknowledging your own mixed feelings with remarks like "The baby sure takes a lot of work and time." Let your children know that you realize this is a difficult time and you know they don't always feel happy; then assure them that they can talk to you about any of their feelings and that you'll understand.

It takes time for everyone in the family to accept completely the arrival of a new baby. Siblings, especially, need time and your understanding to adjust to the change. Knowing what to expect will help you accept your child's negative reactions and it will help assure you that the behaviors are normal adjustment tactics, not signs of a cruel or spoiled child. Try to keep in mind that from your child's point of view, babies are fun people to have visit, but there's no reason for them to stay.

Recommended for further reading:

Siblings Without Rivalry
Adele Faber and Elaine Maclish
Avon, 1988

Chapter Notes

MISTAKE #2

1. Bell, S. M., and M. D. S. Ainsworth. "Infant Crying and Maternal Responsiveness." *Child Development,* 43, pp. 1171–1198.
2. "Why Babies Love Lullabies." *McCall's,* August 1990, p. 25.

MISTAKE #3

1. Shannon, Shelly. "Curses, It's Colic." *Parenting,* August 1990, pp. 82–88.
2. Asnes, Russell S., and Richard L. Mones. "Infantile Colic: A Review." *Developmental and Behavioral Pediatrics,* March 1982, pp. 57–62.
3. O'Donovan, J. D., and A. S. Brenstock. "The Failure of Conventional Drug Therapy in the Management of Infantile Colic." *American Journal of Diseases of Childhood,* 1979, 133, pp. 999–1001.
4. Taubman, Bruce. *Curing Infant Colic.* New York: Bantam Books, 1990.

MISTAKE #4

1. Murray, Ann D. "Infant Crying as an Elicitor of Parental Behavior: An Examination of Two Models." *Psychological Bulletin,* 1979, 86:1, pp. 191–215.

MISTAKE #5

1. Anisfeld, Elizabeth, and Virginia Casper, et al. "Does Infant Carrying Promote Attachment? An Experimental Study of the Effects of Increased Physical Contact on the Development of Attachment." *Child Development,* 1990, 61, pp. 1617–1627.

MISTAKE #7

1. Smith, Barbara A., Thomas J. Fillion, and Elliot M. Blass. "Orally Mediated Sources of Calming in 1- to 3-day-old Human Infants." *Developmental Psychology,* 1990, 26:5, pp. 731–737.

MISTAKE #8

1. Murray, Ann D. "Infant Crying as an Elicitor of Parental Behavior: An Examination of Two Models," *Psychological Bulletin,* 1979, 86:1, p. 201.

MISTAKE #9

1. "Blanketing Insecurity?" *Working Mother,* August 1988, p. 18.

MISTAKE #10

1. Thomas, Alexander, and Stella Chess. *Temperament and Development.* New York: Bruner/Mazel, 1977.

MISTAKE #11

1. Adler, Tina. " 'Melody Is the Message' of Infant-Directed Speech." *APA Monitor,* December 1990, p. 9.
2. Begley, Sharon. "How Far Does the Head Start Go?" *Newsweek,* March 28, 1983, p. 65.

MISTAKE #13

1. Rubenstein, Carin. "Why Don't Dads Do More?" *Working Mother,* June 1990, pp. 55–57.
2. *Ibid.*

MISTAKE #15

1. Elkind, David. *The Hurried Child.* Reading, Massachusetts: Addison-Wesley Publishing Company, 1989.

Index